D1014531

DATE DUE

Christian Jr./Sr High School
2100 Greenfield Dr
El Cajon, CA 92019

POWER TO THE PEOPLE

POWER TO THE PEOPLE

AN AMERICAN STATE AT WORK

TOMMY G. THOMPSON
GOVERNOR OF WISCONSIN

HarperCollins*Publishers*

FIRST EDITION

Designed by C. Linda Dingler
Frontispiece photograph © by Christopher C. Mohrman

Library of Congress Cataloging-in-Publication Data

Thompson, Tommy George, 1941–
    Power to the people : an American state at work / Tommy G. Thompson.
        p.   cm.
    Includes index.
    ISBN 0-06-017823-X
    1. Wisconsin—Politics and government—1951–   2. Wisconsin—Economic policy.   3. Wisconsin—Social policy.   I. Title.
JK6016.T56   1996
320.'9775—dc20   96-24722

96 97 98 99 00 ❖/RRD 10 9 8 7 6 5 4 3 2 1

To Sue Ann, Kelli, Tommi, and Jason

CONTENTS

ACKNOWLEDGMENTS

There are many people who helped make this book possible. This story about Wisconsin's laboratory of democracy could not have been written without the people of Wisconsin, who gave me the opportunity to try our reforms over the past decade and are the ones who really made them work. I am very grateful for their support.

No political leader can achieve much without a strong team of staff and supporters helping along the way. There are so many people who have helped me over the past decade that I can't possibly name everyone here, but I want to say thank you nonetheless. I am indebted to the members of my cabinet, past and present, including, but not limited to, Jim Klauser, Bill McCoshen, Mark Bugher, Carol Skornicka, Chuck Thompson, John Tries, Marlene Cummings, Mike Sullivan, George Meyer, Joe Leean, Dick Dean, Alan Tracy, Moose Speros, Jon Litscher, Ray Boland, Dwight York, Jerry Whitburn, Bruno Mauer, John Torgerson, Tim Cullen, and Bob Trunzo. The ideas in this book and the successful experiments Wisconsin has conducted would not have been possible without their hard work and the work of many other people both in and out of government.

I am indebted to my current staff, including John Matthews, Kevin Keane, and Connie Hagen, as well as to those who were with me during some of our toughest early battles: Christopher Mohrman, Rick Chandler, Patricia Hackett, Tom Fonfara, Bill Jordahl, Diane Harmelink, Scott Jensen, Ave Bie, Jon Henkes, Pat Osborne, Dave Kluesner, Donna Sarow, and Scott Fromader, to name just a few. I am also grateful to Jean Rogers, David Blaska, Jeff Knight, Bob Brandherm, Joe Tregoning, Terry Mulcahy, Dick Lorang, Dick Wegner, Jim Malone, Terry Grosenheider, Ann Agnew, Dean Stensberg, Aleta Murray, Nancy Burke, and so many other dedicated workers in state agencies and in the private sector who have made our reforms work.

There are many friends and supporters who have worked with me over the past decade to change government in Wisconsin. Among them are John MacIver, Sandy MacNeil, and Fred Luber; Lieutenant Governor Scott McCallum; and many members of the state legislature, but especially Betty Jo Nelsen, David Prosser, Susan Engeleiter, Margaret Farrow, Mary Panzer, Mike Ellis, and Joe Andrea. I also want to acknowledge the support of good friends like Butch Johnson, Dennis Markos, and Gene Delmore, who never hesitate to remind me that being governor does not mean you're infallible.

I wish to thank Renae Waterman, who helped me put together my record over ten years as governor. Her research and organizational skills were invaluable. Mark Liedl helped shape my recollections and experiences into a manuscript and put up with my demanding schedule by working with me on many weekends and evenings. I am grateful to Mark, as well as to Beatrice, Christopher, Jonathan, William, and David Liedl, who let me borrow their husband and father. And this book would not have been possible without the guidance and assistance of literary agent Rafe Sagalyn and of Eric Steel, my editor at HarperCollins. They are top-notch professionals who were a pleasure to work with. I particularly thank Eric for his skillful editing; his assistant, Sarah Polen, for keeping us on schedule; and all the staff at HarperCollins for their hard work.

And finally, my own achievements would not have been possible without the support and love from my family. Sue Ann, Kelli, Tommi, and Jason, thank you for putting up with a politician in the family.

A TIME FOR CHANGE

"Y ou have two ears and one mouth. Use them in that proportion and you'll do just fine."

It was one of my father's favorite instructions to me, my sister, and my two brothers, the sort of "Midwestern intellect" I heard often while growing up in the small farming community of Elroy, Wisconsin. It is good advice for anyone, but especially for politicians. I have been the governor of Wisconsin for ten years, and I have always tried to follow that common-sense rule. Now, I'm trying to get Washington to do the same.

Like most Americans, my experience with the federal government has not been particularly pleasant. It is very hard to get Washington to listen. The federal bureaucracy seems impervious to ordinary citizens and governors alike. And yet, it appears to be everywhere, touching more of our everyday lives. Having dealt with Washington on numerous issues over the past decade, I can easily understand why many Americans are fed up with a government they view as increasingly unresponsive, wasteful, and inefficient at solving problems. I'm convinced most government officials in Washington actually have two mouths and one ear.

Since 1986, I have trudged regularly to the nation's capital, asking for more flexibility to make specific changes in federal programs affecting my state. Usually I was met with indifference. I'd have to schedule appointments weeks in advance, only to have a congressman say no to my request for more state-level authority. Even some congressmen from Wisconsin were not that eager to return more decision-making back home. And in most other congressional offices I was treated much like any other supplicant asking for something with very little to offer in return. "Governor who?" the earnest young staffers asked. It was as though Congress couldn't quite figure out how I or forty-nine other governors were relevant to their decision-making.

Asking Washington to give up any amount of control is not a pleasant undertaking. Having dealt with three different presidential administrations, I know the procedure all too well. It essentially means getting down on bended knee and kissing the rings of appointed bureaucrats who have the power to decide whether a governor—duly elected by the citizens of an entire state—can be trusted to change federal programs that clearly are failing. And it has mattered very little whether Democrats or Republicans were in charge. A capital city that runs on the political philosophy of "I can run your life better than you can" naturally fosters a certain arrogance among its inhabitants, regardless of political party. I felt as though Washington had actual contempt for those who didn't live and work inside the Beltway.

But Washington is starting to listen. Now when I visit Capitol Hill, members of Congress actually come out of their offices to greet me. "Tommy, how are you? Good to see you. Have any new ideas?" they ask. And these are just the Democrats.

The American political landscape is beginning to change. After nearly a century of consolidating more and more power in Washington, Congress appears genuinely interested in devolving power back to states and local communities. I know this for sure because on January 12, 1995, I was testifying before the

Senate Labor Committee on the need to overhaul federal job-training programs. As Senator Edward Kennedy began his opening remarks before my testimony, I was bracing for a few partisan shots to the chin.

Instead, the senior senator from Massachusetts said, "I just want to say that we have heard great things about your training program, and that Wisconsin is really one of the outstanding states in terms of these programs. I know from the people whom I respect the most in my state that they have a very high regard for what you have done in Wisconsin. So we are looking forward to hearing from you."

"Great things . . . outstanding . . . looking forward to hearing from" me. I was temporarily speechless. But for the next hour or so we had a cordial, informative discussion about the importance of giving states more flexibility in running job-training programs.

Of course, the cold hard reality of Washington's new willingness to listen stems in large part from the political earthquake that jolted Congress in 1994. In the November elections, thirty-seven incumbent Democrat congressmen were sent packing, defeated in their reelection bids. Republicans took control in both houses of Congress for the first time since 1954. Mindful of this change, Bill Clinton shifted course. In his 1996 State of the Union address, he proudly proclaimed, "The era of big government is over."

But what does that mean? Is it rhetoric or reality? In every presidential election since Lyndon Johnson launched the Great Society, American voters have elected a president who ran against Washington—candidates who decried centralized bureaucracy and promised to change the way the federal government does business. But during these decades Washington continued to grow, assuming more and more power and authority over states, communities, and individuals. The federal budget has grown by 324 percent since 1976, and federal regulations have increased. During the early 1980s, for the first time in our nation's history, more people were employed by government than were working in manufacturing jobs.

Even so, I believe America has reached one of those rare defining moments in history. We are approaching a new millennium. And as we elect a president who will lead us into the next century, the issue of devolving power back to states and communities is picking up steam. Both politically and practically, America is poised for its next great evolution of government: the transfer of power away from Washington and back to the people.

It is time for Washington—its politicians and bureaucrats— to realize they are not paragons of virtue: the states have innovative ideas that work. It is time for them to acknowledge that a one-size-fits-all brand of government handed down from Washington doesn't work today and will not work to meet the challenges of the next century.

America's last major political reform, the Progressive movement, started a century ago in the Republican Party of Wisconsin. It spread first across the Midwest and then many of its ideas were adopted and adapted by Republicans and Democrats. Today, governors—some in the very same states that launched the first Progressive movement—are succeeding with a new wave of innovative reforms and asking Washington to return power and authority to the states. For good reason.

In many ways, what's happening today at the state level is strikingly similar to the grassroots Progressive movement of a century ago. In fact, those today who call for the devolution of power from Washington back to the states are voicing a prominent theme of the early Progressives. Wisconsin Progressive Robert La Follette and his contemporaries strongly believed the states were America's laboratories of democracy. Woodrow Wilson, an early Progressive, warned as governor of New Jersey, "I suspect that the people of the United States understand their own interests better than any group of men in the confines of the country understand them. I don't want a smug lot of experts to sit down behind closed doors in Washington and play providence to me."

After nearly a century of increasing federal authority, this central issue has again risen to the surface of today's political debate. Can people be trusted to govern themselves at the state and local level, or do we need Washington to impose its mandates on all of us?

As we answer that question, America's laboratories of democracy are demonstrating new successes, solving problems where Washington has failed. Successful innovations at the state level are occurring when many of us are sick and tired of the partisan squabbling and arrogance that dominates the federal government. It's no coincidence. People today are trying to work things out closer to home.

Meanwhile, Washington politicians bicker and flex their muscles in partisan contests like filibusters and government shutdowns. As Democrat Senator Bill Bradley of New Jersey said when he retired from the Senate in August 1995,

> The political debate has settled into two familiar ruts. The Republicans are infatuated with the "magic" of the private sector and reflexively criticize government as the enemy of freedom, and the Democrats distrust the market, preach government as the answer to our problems, and prefer the bureaucrat they know to the consumer they can't control. Neither party speaks to people where they live their lives.

While this may be true of Washington, it is a far cry from Wisconsin and other states where government actually is working every day to solve problems in new ways. Although on the national level the political parties may not "speak to people where they live," governors have to, because governors work and live where the people live. Governors who dwell in ideological ruts instead of coming up with real-world solutions aren't around long enough to show off their partisan muscles. People want action, and governors have to deliver.

My intention in this book is to tell the story of one laboratory of democracy that is working to change the relationship
between government and people. It is about devolving power
back from Washington—freeing Wisconsin and other laboratories of democracy from Washington's control so we can do more
of what works for the people of our states. We have created an
approach to governing that is working in Wisconsin, the birthplace of America's Progressive movement. It's an approach I
believe could work elsewhere—even if some, many, or all the
details needed to be adapted to specific, localized situations.
But even if our ideas can work in other states and communities,
Washington is still holding the reins too tightly to allow it to
happen.

I have been elected three times as an unabashedly "pro-
business" governor in a state with a long history of significant
government control over the private sector. I have been an
activist governor who values results over rhetoric. I took on
issues like welfare reform back in 1987 before it was "politically
correct." And I started the nation's first private-school choice
program, allowing low-income children to attend any school
they choose. I am conservative, and a Republican. And I have
had the privilege of serving as governor of Wisconsin longer
than anyone in the state's history.

I have succeeded in Wisconsin not by abandoning my
state's tradition of progressive government, but by building on
it—by trying new solutions, even when it meant directly con-
fronting the philosophy of government that had dominated the
state for a generation. A willingness to experiment with change
and redirect the focus of government was at the heart of
Wisconsin's first Progressive movement. And as was true a century ago, the changes in Wisconsin over the past decade didn't
happen without a fight. But those who fought to preserve the
status quo this time were not the conservatives. My opponents
were Wisconsin liberals who liked to consider themselves "progressives." Yet, the Progressive movement that grew out of

Wisconsin's Republican Party was a meshing of old-fashioned individualism, traditional values, and concern for the needs of the poor and ordinary working people.

Consistent with this tradition, progressive state-level government does not have to be designed around contemporary liberal ideology. I have tapped into the reform-minded roots of my state to create a proactive government designed around conservative values. Our progressive government is one that has changed welfare by requiring individual responsibility from recipients in exchange for assistance. It is a government that empowers ordinary people by cutting their taxes and aggressively promoting economic growth in the private sector so good jobs are available for working people. It breaks up private and public monopolies, creating competition in critical areas like education by allowing low-income families to choose either public or private schools. And it is a government that always balances its budget.

I am not an "anti-government" conservative. I served in the Wisconsin State Legislature for twenty years—it was a part-time job—before being elected governor. From both a philosophical and a practical perspective, I draw a major distinction between the roles of state governments and the role of the federal government. I believe the framers of the Constitution recognized a strong role for state governments, the level of government closer to the people. I do not believe they created or quite envisioned the level of federal power and authority that exists today.

I am not an ideologue. My governing philosophy is common sense. I grew up helping my family run a small grocery store in Elroy, Wisconsin. As governor, I apply an Elroy "grocery store standard" to government solutions. If it won't make sense in the small-town grocery store, it probably won't work. If ordinary people don't understand what government is doing, then what government is doing probably isn't right. Government doesn't have to be complicated. Bureaucrats, politicians, and lobbyists defend its complexity in today's complex world because if government is kept out of the reach of ordinary citizens, they can stay in charge. By self-definition, they become indispensable.

Like other successful governors, I'm a doer. When I ran for a third term in 1994, my campaign theme was "Making It Happen." That is what my job as governor has been all about. And that is what this story of Wisconsin's decade of experimentation with a new kind of progressive government is all about. This is a book for people who are searching for faith in their government, a book informing them of the possibilities, cutting through political rhetoric, and getting down to business.

This is a book about getting things done in the real world. It describes how one governor of one state tackled welfare reform, balanced budgets, and changed the structure and focus of government. It is about commonsense reforms at a level of government closer to the people—about trying new things, experimenting with them in the field. As America searches for ideas that work, *Power to the People* is about one laboratory of democracy that is working.

CHAPTER ONE

GOVERNMENT SENSE VERSUS COMMON SENSE

In 1784, Thomas Jefferson wrote, "Every government degenerates when trusted to the rulers of the people alone." These are words that many in government today seem to have forgotten. The key to America's greatness lies in the good sense of her people, not in the pronouncements of her leaders.

In 1784, it might have been easier to govern the nation from Washington. The population of the new United States was no greater than the population of most individual states today. Granted, communication technology wasn't what it is today, but most everyone lived on the East Coast. Running Washington was not a full-time job. There was no mammoth bureaucracy, no mountain of rules and regulations. Because there was no air-conditioning, there was no worry that politicians and bureaucrats would stay in Washington during the summer. Our elected leaders spent most of their time actually living in the communities they represented.

It is ironic that as our nation has become larger and more diverse, Washington has grown more and more controlling. If mandates from rulers in Washington were not appropriate in 1784, they are even less so today. Americans are not less capable than we were in Jefferson's time (we are certainly more educated), but in its zeal to solve every problem, the federal government has given us what Jefferson feared. Across America, the real-world common sense of ordinary people has been supplanted by "government sense" from Washington, D.C.

In *The Death of Common Sense*, Philip Howard demonstrates how modern-day American government has deliberately sought to eliminate common sense in the areas of everyday life it regulates. Government regulations are purposefully written to eliminate any individual discretion in their application in the real world. Why? Because in a centralized bureaucracy, uniform results are critically important. The government-sense view of the world must anticipate every possible human action and its consequence and make rules to ensure an appropriate outcome of that activity.

So, for example, when the Environmental Protection Agency sets out to prescribe the appropriate uses of one particular chemical, it produces a regulation that is longer than the U.S. Constitution and the Bill of Rights. And under this same government-sense philosophy, it becomes quite rational for the federal government's Occupational Safety and Health Administration to publish one hundred forty separate rules governing the proper use of wooden ladders in the workplace. Replacing common sense requires a lot of regulations.

Almost every day in newspapers across the country, there are examples of the absurd results of Washington's government-sense approach. One recent story involved the U.S. Labor Department and a radio station in Springfield, Missouri. KTOZ-AM, a small station specializing in big-band music, had just reopened after bankruptcy. To make ends meet, the station enlisted volunteer disc jockeys.

The arrangement worked well for the station and the nineteen volunteer disc jockeys ranging in age from twenty-four to seventy-one. For the station, it meant saving enough in salaries to pay for rent and utilities. For the DJs, it was an opportunity to do something they enjoyed, a chance to share their favorite songs with listeners. One of the volunteers, Jerry Kleen, worked the airwaves once a week for four hours, around his regular job at the blue-jeans factory next door to the station. "I'm having fun," he explained. "I know as a rule DJs aren't paid much anyway, so I don't see that I'm losing out on that much."

But the U.S. Labor Department wasn't entertained. Under federal law, volunteers may not work for a for-profit business. They must be paid at least minimum wage, says the Fair Labor Standards Act of 1938.

"The general rule is the employer cannot accept volunteer employment because the obligation is on the employer to pay for it, not on whether the volunteer wants to get paid," said the district director of the Labor Department's Wage and Hour Division to a reporter from the Associated Press.

Speaking from the standpoint of regular American common sense, the station's general manager replied, "As a U.S. citizen, why can't you do with your time what you want? We're not hurting anybody, we're not ripping anybody off. We're bringing a lot of enjoyment to people. What's wrong with that?"

As a governor who has faced an entire battery of federal regulations during the past decade, I can attest to the befuddlement of the station manager. Last year, I submitted to the House Budget Committee a list of more than two hundred unnecessary federal requirements placed on my state by various regulations and mandates. Many of these are unfunded federal mandates, meaning the federal government requires us to administer programs or set up costly enforcement mechanisms without providing the money to do so. Our list was far from exhaustive—the two hundred items we mentioned were just the easy ones to pick out. These unfunded federal regulations cost Wisconsin more than $270 million each year, which is more than our annual welfare payments and more than the cost of operating our entire Department of Natural Resources. I asked Congress to stop micromanaging states and local communities.

"Set broad goals if you need to," I told the committee. "But stop dictating to us how to achieve those goals."

I've seen firsthand how well-intentioned federal regulations that make sense on paper often become ludicrous when they are applied in fifty different states. Federal regulations prohibit landfills within 10,000 feet of airports: birds attracted to landfills might fly into airplanes. This problem may be very real in some states, and regulations to address the situation may be necessary in those areas, but it is certainly not a problem for every airport in all fifty states. Federal officials noticed a violation of this regulation in Door County, Wisconsin, where the county landfill is situated approximately 7,800 feet from the county airport. Door County officials assured their federal counterparts that the gulls at this particular landfill never fly in the direction of the runway. In ten years there had never been a bird-related incident. Moreover, the county landfill had recently been honored as the cleanest, best-managed landfill in the state.

Unsuccessful with this approach—and facing the choice of either moving the landfill or closing the airport—Door County officials spent $23,000 to capture two dozen seagulls from the flocks at the landfill and paint them pink to prove conclusively to federal officials that none of the now clearly identified birds fly in the direction of the airport. It still didn't convince federal officials to bend their rules.

Another example involves timber wolves. For several years we have been working to expand the major north-south highway in northwestern Wisconsin, which runs 150 miles from Eau Claire past Bloomer and Rice Lake and on to Superior, from two lanes to four. Because timber wolves, an endangered species, reside in the forests of the area, the federal government required us to determine the feasibility of special wolf crossings before the highway could be improved. We had our own ideas about how to protect our wolves, and we were working on a plan with our neighboring state of Minnesota, based on its experience. Washington, however, said we had to do it Washington's way. Among other things, we were required to determine the effectiveness of "wolf crossing" signs in the areas where the wolves could safely cross the highway. After two years of delay and $1 million in extra costs, it was determined that the wolves wouldn't use special highway crossings. As anyone in northern Wisconsin will tell you, timber wolves can't read signs.

Every year, my state has lost federal highway funds because we don't have a mandatory helmet law for motorcycles. Wisconsin is the home of Harley-Davidson, and our motorcycle safety record is one of the best in the nation—better than states that have mandatory helmet laws. But our safety record didn't matter to the federal government—it had a rule to enforce.

We also have an innovative tire stockpile reduction program in which Wisconsin companies use old tires to generate energy. A new federal law, however, required us to begin using scrap tire rubber in our asphalt for highways as a way to reduce stockpiles in landfills. This caused two problems. First, asphalt with recycled tires doesn't hold up as well as conventional asphalt in our cold winters and hot summers. Furthermore, the asphalt can't be recycled a second time like regular asphalt. So the end result will be more asphalt in landfills and more road repair and construction. Both the environment and motorists end up losing. The second problem is, we don't have any stockpiles of old tires. Our used tires already are being recycled for other purposes. Complying with the federal regulation meant four hundred jobs could be lost in the three Wisconsin companies that now rely on the shredded tires in their manufacturing process. Plus, if we failed to comply with the federal regulation, the state would lose $18.9 million in federal highway aid, which in part comes from federal gasoline taxes our motorists pay.

In 1995, I testified before Congress about the need to eliminate Washington's motorcycle-helmet and shredded-tire mandates. The Republican Congress listened and passed a bill that year to eliminate the requirements. Washington really is beginning to use its ears.

The bottom line is that many well-intentioned federal regulations fail to achieve their desired goal. A Department of Labor crackdown on station KTOZ in Springfield does nothing to discourage real-world sweatshop labor, which is the intention of the Fair Labor Standards Act. Delaying a Wisconsin highway project did nothing to help the endangered timber wolf, but it did increase costs to taxpayers and mean that people had to travel on a dangerous two-lane highway for a longer period of time. When government sense prevails over common sense, the results are often perverse.

Sometimes Washington's government-sense approach is less obvious, but insidious nonetheless. Last summer I received a press release from the U.S. Department of Transportation announcing its campaign to "stop red light running." Running red lights certainly is a serious matter, but why is the federal government involved? Common sense would suggest it should be a matter for local law enforcement. But the federal government is involved because it has an agency, the Federal Highway Administration, that is charged with promoting highway safety. And since the federal government collects tax revenue from citizens and businesses in the fifty states to help fund the activities of such federal agencies, it understandably decides to spend some of those tax revenues on grants to local communities to stop red light running. But wouldn't it be better to keep those tax revenues in the states and communities in the first place and let them decide how and even if they will spend their own dollars on stopping red light running?

And yet, there seems very little that politicians, much less ordinary Americans, can do about Washington's meddling. The federal bureaucracy seems impervious to common sense, continually assuming more responsibility and imposing more of its "solutions" on states, communities, and individuals.

As long as power remains centralized in Washington,

government sense will continue to reign. But as many governors, state legislators, mayors, and local elected officials know too well, the one-size-fits-all approach of regulations from Washington fails to suit the realities of different states and communities across the nation. Simply put, our highly centralized approach to government is too inflexible to be effective in today's society. Surely no one would disagree that it is appropriate for government to ensure safe air travel, but when it means local officials have to paint birds pink to prove a point, something is drastically wrong.

Common sense cannot flourish in an America where Washington calls all the shots. As long as power remains centralized in Washington, the balance of power between government and individuals will remain askew. Federal bureaucrats are working in a system built on the philosophy that they can manage your life better than you can. And so, quite naturally, for them to do a better job managing your life, they need to manage more and more of it.

For that to change, the underlying system that grants Washington dominant authority must be reexamined. America's experience, particularly over the past three decades, demonstrates that if Washington has the authority, 535 members of Congress and nearly 3 million federal bureaucrats will find a way to use it. Over the past thirty years, the Washington establishment has proven fiercely resistant to incremental changes. Only a fundamental devolution of power from Washington will restore the balance of responsibilities between government and individuals.

By no means are state and local governments immune to this natural tendency of government to assume more power. Yet these governments are closer to the people they are supposed to serve. That proximity, as the framers of the Constitution understood, acts as a natural check on government power. In a real sense, it acts to ensure that the common sense of ordinary people will not be supplanted by the government sense of a distant, insulated elite. A key to restoring commonsense government, therefore, is to breathe life into the framework established in the Constitution under the Tenth Amendment: "The powers not delegated to the United States by the Constitution, nor prohibited by it to the States, are reserved to the States respectively, or to the people."

The Tenth Amendment reserves power not just to the states but to the people themselves. Replacing one large Washington government with fifty greatly expanded states governments may be an improvement, but it's not a solution.

Government sense is not exclusively Democrat or Republican. It's easy to point fingers, but both political parties and all levels of government are equally capable of settling into the ruts. I think most everyone—Democrats and Republicans, men and women who don't align themselves with any party—wants to see good jobs for workers and wants to help people get off welfare. They want children to receive the best education. They want to be safe from crime and able to appreciate and enjoy the country around them. Invariably we disagree on how to make those things come about, and, over time, constructive disagreement can become partisan debate. To me, the smart choice is to do what works. The labels don't matter all that much. It's common sense.

ELROY COMMON SENSE

Everyone has his or her own common sense. Mine is rooted in the values I learned growing up in the small Wisconsin community of Elroy.

In the 1940s and 1950s, people in Elroy generally had a positive view of the federal government, but we didn't have much contact with it in our everyday lives. We were a self-sufficient community. We didn't need Washington or anyone else to tell us to work hard, support our families, and look after our neighbors. Our families, schools, and churches taught us that, and the tightness of the community reinforced those fundamental values. You would have found the same was true in countless towns and big-city neighborhoods throughout America.

We've lost a good part of that self-reliance and sense of community in America today. As sociologist James Q. Wilson has noted, "Today we expect 'government programs' to accomplish what families, villages and churches once accomplished."

My mother and father were both schoolteachers. They met in Elroy's two-room schoolhouse. My father taught the upper grades in one room and my mother taught the lower grades in the other room. After a few years, they got married. Politically, my parents were independents, although my mother voted Democrat more often than my father. Both had been influenced by the Progressive Party that grew out of the Republican Party in Wisconsin during the first part of the century. They shared the Progressive view of government as a powerful force for positive change.

It was easy for them to share Progressive ideals as far as most people were concerned, because these ideals were not specific to either political party: people should be trusted, government can be a catalyst for positive change, and a larger power should be controlled if it robs individual people of the power to control their own lives.

My mother, Julie, was Irish Catholic. She was the most compassionate and caring person I've ever known. She was always reaching out to help people and making sure I did the same. My mother instilled in me a sense a service toward others. She used to tell me that I should never be too tired to go out and help someone less fortunate or to be willing to volunteer and serve.

Allan Thompson, my father, was a practical, commonsense German American. He believed very strongly in the work ethic and in individuals taking responsibility for themselves and their actions. He required respect and took a no-nonsense approach to most everything.

When I was sixteen years old, I talked back to one of my

teachers and was promptly sent home from school for the day. My father turned me right around and marched me up to the high school to apologize to the teacher in front of my entire class (which, at fifty-five students, comprised a good share of Elroy's population). But even that wasn't enough for my father. That same evening, I was dispatched to the local school board meeting to apologize to them. I never lipped off to a teacher again.

Soon after he and my mother married, my father quit teaching and opened up a grocery store in Elroy. I started working in the store when I was six years old. I had wanted a new bike, so he put me to work polishing eggs and sweeping floors at 25 cents an hour to earn the money. The lesson was very clear: If you wanted something you had to work for it. (Nearly fifty years later, the *New York Times Magazine* wrote a story about my successful welfare reforms in Wisconsin. The title was "Governor 'Get-A-Job.'" My father would've been proud.)

I learned much about people working in the Thompson grocery store, and I learned about government there too. On Friday nights, the area farmers and civic leaders would gather in the store for regular discussions. My father served on the county board, so people would come into the store to discuss politics and government. If someone had a problem with a road or some government service that wasn't being done right, he'd come in and talk to my dad. He would go out and take a look at the problem or make a phone call and try to solve it. No cumbersome bureaucratic process, no reams of paperwork. This was, without a doubt, government solving problems. It was effective, grassroots, American government.

That image of government has never left me. It worked. Government was a partner in the community—in fact, it was an actual person, elected by the voters, whom people could talk to and trust to actually solve problems and get things done. When people had a problem within my father's jurisdiction, they didn't go to Mauston, the county seat, they went to the Thompson grocery store. There was Allan Thompson, who would look them in the eye, listen to their problem, and then go out and do something about it.

During my senior year of high school, I applied to the West Point Academy and the University of Wisconsin at Madison. I wasn't accepted at West Point, so I left home in 1959 to attend college at the University of Wisconsin at Madison, where the size of my freshman class was double the population of my hometown. Like many kids who grew up in small towns, I hadn't realized I was poor until I left Elroy. I enrolled in ROTC and worked at a restaurant and then as a bartender to pay my tuition. My first major foray into politics came in 1963 when I helped organize Barry Goldwater's presidential campaign on the University of Wisconsin campus. It was, to say the least, a major challenge. Madison was a hotbed of radical politics, and supporting Barry Goldwater certainly bucked the conventional campus wisdom. But I had read his book *Conscience of a Conservative*, and it made a lot of sense to me. And to be honest, I also enjoyed the prospect of challenging the university establishment.

During my senior year, I accepted an internship on Capitol Hill. I listened to a lot of famous people give speeches that summer—including Bobby Kennedy. But the person who impressed me the most was Jimmy Hoffa. He was not a big man, but he had a presence and a forcefulness and a straight-talking style that took over the room when he spoke. Normally, the other interns and I would listen to the speakers with varying degrees of interest, but with Hoffa, it seemed as if we were compelled to listen. He spoke without notes for forty-five minutes, and none of us missed a word.

Upon returning from Washington I enrolled in law school at the University of Wisconsin, determined to run for political office someday. It happened sooner than I thought. In 1966, during my third year of law school, I decided to challenge the state representative from my home district. He was a Republican, and a sixteen-year incumbent. I didn't think I would win, but I wanted to get my name known in the district so I could run when he retired. I was planning to run in the election and then enlist in the Air Force Judge Advocate General program.

As fate would have it, the incumbent made the mistake of taking a two-week cruise to Alaska shortly before the primary election. With a $100 car and $10 a day from my father—$5 for gas and $5 for food—I spent twenty-one days knocking on every door in the district. By the time my opponent returned from Alaska and realized what was happening, it was too late.

I spent the next twenty years serving in the assembly of Wisconsin's part-time legislature and practicing law in the district. I married Sue Ann Mashak and we set about raising our three children in Elroy. By 1981, I had risen to minority leader in the state assembly, where I earned the moniker "Dr. No" for my role in blocking proposals advanced by the liberal majority.

As the 1986 gubernatorial election approached, the incumbent Democrat, Tony Earl, was in trouble. The state ranked fortieth in the nation in job growth, welfare rolls were high, and state spending and taxes were out of control.

I ran in the Republican primary for governor much as I had run for the state legislature twenty years earlier: by getting in the car and meeting and listening to as many people as I could. According to surveys commissioned by better-funded candidates at the start of the primaries, only 3 percent of the voters around the state had heard of me, so I opened each speech by telling people, "Yes, my real name is Tommy, not Thomas, and yes, I come from Elroy, Wisconsin."

Hardly anyone knew where Elroy was, so I would explain, "Elroy is a small community located between Kendall and Union Center, north of Wonewoc and south of Hustler." Of course, those four communities were even smaller and less well known than Elroy, so it always elicited a laugh. It was a good way to break the ice and get people's attention so I could talk about serious issues. But it also told people that where I come from says a lot about who I am and what I believe in.

I hired John Tries, an ex-policeman from Milwaukee, as my driver, and together we traveled across the state listening and talking to people. I went everywhere, to small towns where no candidate for governor had ever visited and to union halls and the central city, where Republican candidates weren't supposed to go. I talked with and listened to people in the taverns and the barbershops and the dairy barns and learned a lot about what people were thinking. I had some ideas about what I would do as governor, but I got many more good ones from listening. Since few people knew who I was, I accepted almost every invitation I received to go speak to a group or attend a candidate forum. One Sunday, John and I drove four hours one way to an event in a remote county. We were told that if you wanted to win the election in that county, this was the place to go. When we arrived, there were four people present, one for every hour we had driven.

My campaign didn't have much money, so John and I would share a room in the cheapest hotels we could find. Motel 6 was well beyond our reach. These hotels were interesting places. I'll never forget one in particular, in Waupun, which had a plastic laminated sign on the phone with instructions on "how to use the phone." Line 1 of the instructions said, "Do not answer the phone unless it rings." (Clearly, they were not big believers in common sense.)

I surprised the experts by winning a five-candidate GOP primary with 52 percent of the vote. I ran in the general election on a platform of cutting taxes, controlling spending, reforming welfare, and creating an economic climate of opportunity for businesses and individuals. I knew our high taxes, out-of-control spending, welfare system, and failing economy were the most important issues because I heard it firsthand from the people. But I didn't just ask about the problems—I asked for solutions. And I really listened to each and every suggestion I received. We took all of these ideas and came up with policy proposals that I believed could really turn our state around. My opponent dismissed me as a "right-wing Republican" and warned of "trickle-down" economics and the abandonment of Wisconsin's "progressive tradition."

In 1986, Republicans did not fare so well around the country. Nationally, the GOP lost control of the U.S. Senate, which it had captured on Ronald Reagan's coattails in 1980. Closer to home, three Democrat governors were reelected in the neighboring states of Minnesota, Michigan, and Ohio. I thought it was a good year: at age forty-four, I was elected governor of Wisconsin.

Four years later, I was reelected, and in January 1994, after seven years of often controversial leadership, I became the longest-serving governor in Wisconsin history. In November 1994, when Democrat incumbents in Washington were being ousted in record numbers, I was reelected to a third four-year term with 67 percent of the vote—the largest margin in modern state history. I carried seventy-one of Wisconsin's seventy-two counties, won approximately 30 percent of the African American vote, and became the first Republican governor in fifty years to win the Democrat stronghold of Milwaukee.

COMMONSENSE GOVERNMENT

I believe my success as governor is the result of my commitment to the commonsense values I learned growing up in Elroy. I think of my office as the corner grocery store where people would go to ask my father for help. As governor, if I see a problem, I go out and fix it, just as Allan Thompson did from his small-town grocery store. And I'm still trying to use my two ears and one mouth in the proper proportion as my father instructed.

More than any governor before me, I have gotten out of the office and traveled around the state—just as I did when I first campaigned for governor. My political opponents have derided me for this, calling me "traveling Tommy." They don't know how much they're not learning by sitting at their desks in the state capitol. My best ideas have come from the commonsense advice of ordinary people. My father was right. There is so much to be learned from listening to real people in the real world.

I remember talking about my approach in one of the first press interviews I gave right after being elected governor. Although I knew I was the most conservative governor Wisconsin had had in a long time, I explained that I planned to lead a very active administration that would respond to the needs of the people without restricting the growth of the private sector. I wanted to make it clear that I wasn't going to let partisanship get in the way of making practical, commonsense decisions for the state of Wisconsin.

The Democrats, who controlled both houses of the state legislature at the time, expected me to be very hostile. To them I was "Dr. No," the Republican minority leader in the state assembly who consistently fought against many of their proposals. So one of the first things I did after I was sworn in as governor was to have Bill Jordahl and Pat Osborne of my staff personally visit each of the legislators in their offices. They were surprised and appreciative.

My next ten years as governor were not without fierce partisan battles over taxes and spending, welfare, education, and crime, but we always have managed to maintain a level of respect and cordiality. In states like Wisconsin, we don't take partisan politics as seriously as they do in Washington. We can fight like cats and dogs over a major policy issue and have a beer after it's over. Part of this is due to our tradition of progressive government—a shared belief that government should get things done. It also reflects the fact that government is only a small part of what goes on in a state. In Washington, government is everything. In a state like Wisconsin, most people don't work for government and are more concerned with raising their children, working hard at their jobs, and watching the Green Bay Packers on Sunday. It gives you a better perspective on politics when your community is not dominated by it.

CHAPTER TWO

A NEW PROGRESSIVE ERA

Much has been written lately about the coming of a second Progressive movement in America. But the people promoting this Progressive resurgence all seem to be political liberals. Their Progressive agenda is nothing new. It is the same old approach we've tried for the past sixty years, dressed up with new buzzwords. Strip it down and you see the same old things—more power to Washington and less to states, communities, and individuals.

What really would be progressive is transferring authority and decision-making away from Washington to the state and local level. Genuine progress would be a government that works in partnership with people to solve problems, promotes individual responsibility rather than displaces it, and demands less in taxes but delivers better quality services. It would be flexible, responsive, practical government.

Let's face it. There is nothing "progressive" about the old model of centralized Washington, D.C., bureaucracy. Today's progressives are the activist governors, legislators, and mayors who are ignoring Washington's one-size-fits-all solutions. They are challenging the status quo by asking for the flexibility and authority to experiment with new ideas and new approaches that will work best in their own communities.

In fact, today's liberal philosophy has more in common with the New Deal and Lyndon Johnson's Great Society than with the original Progressive movement. The early Progressives believed in state-based experimentation, while liberals believed in Washington-based control. The early Progressives passed reforms that returned power to ordinary people, while many liberals supported policies that substituted government authority for individual responsibility. Liberals claimed the Progressive mantle but undermined many of its fundamental tenets by replacing decision-making by states, communities, and individuals with a massive new bureaucracy in Washington, D.C. As Progressive journalist Mark Sullivan wrote in 1935 in reaction to the New Deal, "The enemy was regimentation attempted by big business. The enemy now is regimentation attempted by government."

Although there was a wide variety of ideological strains in America's Progressive movement, many of its original proponents espoused views very similar to those of contemporary conservatives. As historian Richard Hofstadter notes in *The Age of Reform*, "Progressivism, at its heart, was an effort to realize traditional and familiar ideals under novel circumstances." For example, the Progressive battles against private sector monopolies expressed traditional free-market values of competition and entrepreneurship. And President Theodore Roosevelt, a Republican, called Progressivism the "highest and wisest form of conservatism."

America's turn-of-the-century Progressive movement started in the Republican Party of Wisconsin. Republicans like Robert "Fighting Bob" La Follette were fed up with ineffective government. Government at the time was unresponsive to the needs of ordinary working people. It was dominated by special interests dedicated to preserving the status quo. Wisconsin Progressives introduced the then radical notion that government should be responsive to ordinary people rather than a small elite and play an active roll in helping working people. So they established the referendum, the primary, and the recall as tools for citizens to take back their government. They pioneered a new relationship between government and the people it is supposed to serve. We became the first state in the nation to establish worker protections like unemployment insurance and workers compensation.

Wisconsin Progressives used government to develop commonsense solutions to everyday problems. In the book *The Wisconsin Idea*, Theodore Roosevelt described the state's Progressive approach:

> As soon as they decided that a certain object was desirable they at once set to work practically to study how to develop the constructive machinery through which it could be achieved. This is not an easy attitude to maintain. Yet every true reformer must maintain it.

But what started as state-based grassroots reform was hijacked by those who believed in centralized, bureaucratic decision-making. Among the major proponents of this national government approach was Herbert Croly. He summed up his philosophy of government by saying, "The average American individual is morally and intellectually inadequate to a serious and consistent conception of his responsibilities as a democrat." (Mr. Croly would not have been well received in Elroy.) To Croly and the liberals who began calling themselves Progressives, "progress" had two tracks. They promised to improve our lives—but they believed ordinary people would be better off with "enlightened bureaucrats" and "national experts" making the decisions. It's not too hard to see how their model of government essentially became the federal system we have today.

Yet, at its heart, early Progressivism assailed the centralization of power that characterizes American government today. "What I fear," Woodrow Wilson said,

> is a government of experts. God forbid that in a democratic country we should resign the task and give government

over to experts. What are we if we are to be scientifically taken care of by a small number of gentlemen who are the only men to understand the job? Because if we don't understand the job, we are not a free people.

To many early Progressives, the traditional American belief in individual responsibility over government responsibility was a core value, a value that was all but obliterated by liberal Progressives. As Progressive editor and writer George Creel wrote in his 1935 autobiography, "We have fallen from the heights . . . the progressivism preached and led by Theodore Roosevelt, La Follette and Wilson was intensely American—its core a love of country and pride in free institutions. Present-day 'liberalism' as it has the impudence to call itself, is anti American. . . . Not in all history has a word been so wrenched away from its true meaning." I could go on, but Mr. Creel only got angrier.

Although Woodrow Wilson as president would later align himself more closely with the liberal vein of Progressivism, many of the original Progressives fought bitterly against the liberalization of Progressivism as personified by the New Deal. To many Progressives, the class warfare elements of New Deal liberalism struck at the heart of the movement they had created. They viewed it as creating a new political machine at the national level, doling out favors to new special interests.

The New Deal was a victory for those who believed that centralized government could best solve the problems of society. The Great Society expanded that centralization with enormous new social programs at the federal level. And yet today we have something Herbert Croly, Franklin Roosevelt, and Lyndon Johnson didn't have: the invaluable benefit of experience. We have seen their theories in practice. We have seen what works and doesn't work in the real world. And now we have field-tested models—in Wisconsin and elsewhere—that offer viable alternatives to the Washington approach. We can learn from the successes and failures of each approach to create a new model for governing America in the next century.

In one sense, the liberals are right. We do need a new Progressive movement—with the energy and passion of the first one—but one that also reflects what experience has taught us about the dangers and inefficiencies of the centralized government that have emerged. Historian Russell Nye wrote that the first Progressive movement was "rooted in the political and economic soil of the time." The next Progressive movement should be as well, not rooted in the exhausted ground of 1935 or 1965.

THE NEXT PROGRESSIVE MOVEMENT

The time is ripe for a Progressive movement that springs from the contemporary experiences and reforms of America's states, just as the first one did. In 1996, the challenges American government faces and the grassroots response to those challenges are strikingly similar to those in 1896.

The progressive challenge today is really the same. Only there is a different elite that has grown too powerful and too disconnected from the realities of everyday life in our communities. The first Progressives took power back from a private sector elite that had grown too controlling. Now we need to take power from a government sector elite that has grown too controlling.

The first Progressive movement took off when Progressive Republicans gained control of state and local governments in Wisconsin and elsewhere in the Midwest. They began making changes in their own states that challenged the way government operated at the time.

Although record numbers of congressional incumbents were defeated in 1994, several innovative governors around the Midwest were reelected by wide margins: governors like John Engler in Michigan, George Voinovich in Ohio, Terry Branstad in Iowa, Jim Edgar in Illinois, and Arne Carlson in Minnesota. In fact, some of the most popular and longest-serving governors in the nation today come from states with a rich tradition of Progressive politics. They are "activist" governors who have combined conservative values with a can-do attitude that has made government in their states more responsive and effective in solving real-world problems. As such, they have tapped into their states' Progressive traditions of innovative government unafraid to experiment with change. And they are succeeding in solving problems where Washington has failed.

DECENTRALIZED GOVERNMENT

Much of the reform Wisconsin has achieved over the past decade has been based on a rejection of modern liberalism and its model of Washington-based government. A genuine Progressive movement for the next century would return power and authority from Washington to the states and communities. Reviving self-government across the nation will only occur through a rejection of the liberal philosophy expressed by Herbert Croly that "the average American individual is morally and intellectually" incapable of governing himself or herself. Although the statement sounds outrageous, it essentially is how the federal government is set up today. Power will not be restored to the people unless more decision-making is transferred to a level of government closer to the people.

That is an incredibly difficult task. I once helped my son build a model airplane. "Helped" isn't really the right word. I read the instructions. I put the pieces together, glued the wings, and painted the insignias. My son watched. He hadn't learned anything and I hadn't helped. If only there had been instructions before the instructions.

The Founding Fathers wrote instructions. They're called the Constitution. And they're supposed to be read before we follow any other instructions.

There's one very crucial part of these instructions, the Tenth Amendment, which we all too often forget. It reads: "The powers not delegated to the United States by the Constitution, nor prohibited by it to the States, are reserved to the States respectively, or to the people."

The Tenth Amendment was central to the framers' concept of self-government. It limited the federal government to only those powers specifically enumerated in the Constitution and reiterated their central belief that power and authority resided with individuals and their local governments, subject to specific limited exceptions. The framers, after all, established the United *States* of America, not the United *State* of America.

America needs a clash of ideas among the fifty states—the true laboratories of democracy. I want to compete with Governors Pataki in New York, Whitman in New Jersey, Wilson in California, Miller in Nevada, Bush in Texas, Leavitt in Utah, Beasley in South Carolina, Merrill in New Hampshire, and the other governors in an environment that fosters innovation and in which states can freely adopt the best practices that make the most sense for their people. For this to happen, there must be full and open experimentation in the states. Washington must cut the apron strings and allow states the freedom to fully pursue innovative solutions to long-standing problems. Our track record shows we will succeed.

Returning power to the states will give people more authority to control their own government, which was a central goal of the early Progressives. State government is closer to the problems it's attempting to solve, and state-based politicians are more accessible and fundamentally more accountable to citizens. It will also restore our national heritage of trusting the common sense of ordinary Americans rather than dictating government sense from a distant capital.

FLEXIBILITY AND INNOVATION

Flexibility and innovation will be the hallmarks of successful government in the next century. This will require practical approaches to solving problems rather than the partisan and ideologically rigid approaches that mark much of Washington government today. Unlike Washington, governors cannot afford to become bogged down in ideological stalemates. We must govern—come up with actual solutions to real-life problems faced by real people in our states. During the last ten years, I have learned that ideology is essential for developing ideas for more effective public policy, but what people really want and deserve is positive, tangible results. A rigid, philosophically correct policy may not work in the real world at a given time. Political leaders must have the courage to experiment with what works and be flexible enough to alter or discard what doesn't.

This willingness to experiment with new ideas characterized the early Progressives. And my approach has been like that of the earlier Wisconsin Progressives who developed solutions that were specific and practical, not abstract and ideological.

Both politically and operationally, America's Washington-based government stifles innovation and precludes flexibility. Our federal government is based on an outdated model that will be ineffective in meeting the challenges of the next century. But if you look beyond the forest at the trees, you will see that real-world models of flexible, innovative government can be found in states and communities around the country, succeeding where Washington has failed.

Real reform in America has usually come from the bottom up. And so it is today, where most successful policy innovations are happening down the street, in the town or state next door, not in Washington. America's laboratories of democracy truly are today's catalysts and proving grounds for new solutions in critical areas like welfare, education, the economy, protecting the environment, and balancing budgets. If we want a government that can help meet the challenges and realize the opportunities of the next millennium, we need to move away from Washington command and control.

INDIVIDUAL RESPONSIBILITY

In ten years of experimenting with new approaches to government, I have learned that responsibility vested in individuals, families, and communities works better than responsibility vested in government. I believe much of the current failure of government is due to a misappropriation of responsibilities between government and individuals. The welfare system doesn't work because government has all the responsibility and welfare recipients have virtually none. Our nation's education system is failing because bureaucrats have more authority than parents and classroom teachers. Our economy is underproductive because government has consumed too much of the private sector's role. And we have a massive budget deficit because the federal government has assumed all these responsibilities while being utterly irresponsible about the bottom line.

Many of Wisconsin's successful reforms over the past decade have been rooted in reasserting the primacy of individual responsibility. My philosophy presumes that individuals will act responsibly and that in their doing so, the highest benefits for society will be achieved. And in cases in which contemporary government has displaced individual responsibility—such as in the current welfare system—state government in Wisconsin has actively promoted individual responsibility to help people help themselves.

MARKET-BASED SOLUTIONS

My reforms in Wisconsin also have recognized the primacy of market-based decisions. In my view, a truly progressive government works as a partner with business to help create more and better jobs for working people. It does not dictate economic priorities to the private sector, but serves as a catalyst to promote economic growth by cutting taxes and reducing government regulation. Like the early Progressives, I believe very strongly in the extraordinary value of free-market competition. The early Progressives fought against monopolies not because they were anti-business, but because they wanted to restore competitive conditions in the American economy. And just as the early Progressives fought business monopolies, I see modern-day Progressives dismantling private and public sector monopolies. As such, I have enacted reforms in Wisconsin such as private-school choice to improve education by injecting competition into a government-run monopoly. Like other states, we are deregulating our utility industry, and we were among the first states to deregulate telecommunications.

I do not buy into the liberals' profound mistrust of the private sector. Government has a role to play with reasonable regulation, but government's primary role is not to redistribute wealth. A free market unfettered by government interference offers the best avenue of opportunity for the most people. This view was shared by early Progressive leaders such as Theodore Roosevelt, who said that "we must draw the line at misconduct, not against wealth." It was not the Progressives but the liberals who put America squarely on the road to the class warfare that dominates much of national politics today.

THE AGENDA IN ACTION

Over the past decade, Wisconsin has experimented with radical changes in the relationship between government and citizens. Like the early Progressives, we have experimented with different reforms—in welfare, education, job creation, and tax cuts—to determine what works in the real world. We have had successes and failures—but still we have fashioned new relationships between people and government and created new approaches to solve pressing social problems.

To be sure, Wisconsin is not Shangri-la. We still have problems. But among America's laboratories of democracy, the state has a proven record of solutions on tough issues that Washington hasn't handled well. Maybe we've just been at it longer than most states. Or maybe there really is something special going on here.

CHAPTER THREE

WORK NOT WELFARE

DISMANTLING WASHINGTON'S WELFARE SYSTEM

Perhaps no other federal program is more illustrative of the government-sense approach to solving problems than the welfare system, officially known as Aid to Families with Dependent Children (AFDC). Over time, a program that was created to help widows with children get back on their feet has evolved into something altogether different. To achieve "predictable results," rules were written, added to, and rewritten. Today, the regulations governing the federal welfare program stand four feet high, and the typical welfare worker spends 80 percent of his or her time doing paperwork and only 20 percent of the time actually working with people on welfare. The system is broken. It pays people not to work, not to get married, and to have more illegitimate children.

Multiple layers of government bureaucracy consume much of the money taxpayers contribute to help the poor. In fact, if all the money federal, state, and local governments spend this year on welfare simply was given directly to the needy, we would raise every single poor person in America out of poverty more than *two times over*. Our welfare tax dollars are funding a "poverty industry" in America more than they are helping low-income families get ahead.

Given this clear record of failure and the incredible fact that liberals and conservatives both agree the current system isn't working, common sense says Washington would be eager to scrap the system. Instead, the federal government has erected substantial barriers.

Governors who want to try something new must get permission from Washington through an expensive and time-consuming "waiver" process. To experiment with changes in welfare—like requiring recipients to work—states have to prepare a written proposal and submit it to the federal Department of Health and Human Services (HHS). The request must explain what you want to change and why, identify all the federal regulations your reform will affect, set up a procedure for measuring results, and show that the project will not cost the federal government any additional money. It sounds fairly reasonable. The problem is, federal bureaucrats have their own views on what you're really trying to accomplish and why, what federal regulations you're impacting, and how you should measure the results. Any difference of opinion in any one of those parts of the waiver request can tie up the process for months in back-and-forth negotiations, or ultimately doom your request if you can't convince them to see it your way.

For example, when I want to change welfare, my staff has to comb through all the federal welfare regulations, food stamp regulations, and Medicaid regulations just to identify for Washington which of its rules we might be running afoul of. This alone can be a very time-consuming job for state workers who should be doing other things. When our review is submitted, though, HHS bureaucrats may have their own opinions on what federal regulation we are affecting. They may say, "Well, you're not really impacting this rule," or "You left out this regulation." It's entirely subjective. So we spend weeks debating back and forth, submitting and resubmitting the proposal. It makes you want to tear your hair out, but you can't get mad, because they might say no.

If Washington does grant a waiver, it usually amounts to far less of a reform than what was originally requested and what the state legislature has approved. I know, because since I became governor in 1987, Wisconsin has negotiated more welfare waivers than any other state—172 waivers of federal regulations from three different administrations. Although we successfully navigated Washington's waiver minefield, our reforms have been more costly and less effective because of Washington's unwillingness to give up control. Some states are thwarted from even trying reforms because of the daunting obstacles the federal government imposes.

My experience with Washington and the reforms we've implemented in Wisconsin leads me to one overwhelming conclusion. The only real solution to the welfare mess is to scrap the current federal system and allow states to experiment freely with new approaches that will work best for them. Finding effective alternatives to a program that has been in place for more than sixty years is not easy. It is even more difficult because of the nature of the undertaking. Unlike building roads or delivering the mail, helping people act responsibly and become self-sufficient requires creative, person-to-person approaches. Washington is not suited for that. After three generations of tinkering with welfare, Washington must now get out of the way and let America's laboratories of democracy create innovative and flexible solutions that will work in each and every state in our diverse nation.

In fact, *reform* is the wrong word because it suggests adjusting the current system to make it work better. It doesn't work. Welfare as we know it is fundamentally and unalterably destructive. As Franklin Roosevelt described it in 1935, welfare is "a narcotic, . . . a subtle destroyer of the human spirit." The desire to be of help to people in need—that is a good and noble principle, but from it proceeded flawed operating principles of

Washington-based command and control through the dense layers of unworkable regulations and such perverse incentives as rewarding nonwork. The system as it exists today is a behemoth. It cannot be reformed; it needs to be scrapped. The federal government cannot knock the giant over. Bill Clinton promised to change it but has failed to do so.

Over the past decade Wisconsin has changed some of the fundamental premises upon which the current welfare system is based. In doing so, we have altered government's expectations of welfare recipients, the attitude of recipients and welfare workers toward welfare, and, ultimately, the behavior of people receiving assistance. Our changes have been rooted in one overriding principle: government should require individual responsibility in exchange for assistance. We have changed welfare by expecting more from the people who are on it. We expect them to act responsibly, and we actively enforce responsible behavior when necessary. We have changed government to make it a force for promoting individual responsibility among welfare recipients.

Wisconsin began welfare reform in earnest in 1987, before it was the dominant national issue it is today. As we began to demonstrate real-world success of what at the time were "radical" reforms, the national debate on welfare soon began to change. Our successes helped spur movement in Washington and other states for similar reforms. We started out with small experiments and targeted reforms. In 1996, we became the nation's first state to eliminate welfare altogether.

When I was first running for governor, riding from town to town asking people what they wanted me to do if I was elected, changing welfare was high on most everyone's list. The overwhelming refrain from working people was, "People on welfare should have to work." Wisconsin's welfare benefits at the time were the third highest in the nation, and higher than those of our neighboring states. Jobs and working people were leaving the state because our economy was so bad, but welfare recipients were moving in because our benefits were so high. The percentage of the state's population on welfare was growing. It increased threefold from 1970 to 1986, from 2 percent to 6 percent. The number of teenage girls on AFDC increased by 16 percent from 1977 to 1985, and families were staying on welfare longer than ever before. From 1979 through 1985, state spending on AFDC had grown 108 percent, versus a 26 percent increase nationwide. We ranked eighth in the nation in percentage of households on welfare.

During a campaign stop in Milwaukee, a young woman came up to me and put her hand on my arm. She looked at me and pleaded, "Please do something about welfare, it's killing us." She and her two children were on welfare. She wanted to get off welfare and give them a future, but she didn't know how. She felt trapped by it. I heard similar stories from other people I talked to who were on welfare. They wanted to change it as much as—perhaps even more than—the working people who resented paying for the program. Many needed help, and they knew it, but they weren't getting it from welfare. Sure, there were freeloaders who were "scamming" the system, but there were others who wanted to get off welfare and couldn't. They didn't have any work experience. They had no one to help take care of their children. If they showed some initiative and got a job, it often paid less than welfare. And if they went to work, they usually gave up the free health care welfare provided to them and their children. After a while, many of them just accepted welfare as a way of life—they stayed on welfare and raised their children in a home where no one got up in the morning to go to work.

Our own welfare offices were part of the problem. One young woman had gone to the welfare office looking for temporary help and ended up raising her son on welfare. She had been working as a waitress in supper clubs, making good tips. Then she got pregnant, moved in with her mother, and went to the welfare office just before she was due. She wanted help for "a couple of months." The welfare office told her she could sign up, start getting checks immediately, and wouldn't have to come back for another appointment for six months. She came back with her five-month-old son and reported that her mom had agreed to look after the baby while she searched for work, and she probably could get her old job back. "You don't need to do that," her welfare worker said. "The rules say you can stay home, and you don't have to keep living at your mother's. You're eligible for subsidized housing." "Oh really," the young woman said. "Well, OK." She was hooked—she had come in looking for a couple months of help, but the system had sucked her in. This is what Franklin Roosevelt meant when he called welfare a "subtle destroyer." We were helping people into dependency.

During the campaign I put together a task force of individuals from government and the private sector to develop policy proposals on welfare reform and other issues. My reputation as "Dr. No" in the legislature meant the media and most of the political establishment thought I was the guy who could throw a monkey wrench into the works to stop things, but not someone who could put together a program and make it work. I just hadn't had the opportunity.

The task force met every week or so in Milwaukee. John MacIver, a Milwaukee attorney who had worked for Richard Nixon, chaired the group, along with Jim Klauser, who had worked with state government for years and was my top campaign adviser. The group included state legislators Betty Jo Nelsen, David Prosser, and Don Stitt; business leaders such as Mary Kohler, Bruno Mauer, Sandy MacNeil, and Tom Hefty; and my legislative assistant Rick Chandler. I would tell Rick or Jim Klauser what I was hearing on the campaign trail and what I wanted to do, and they would bring it to the group for more research and discussion. Rick usually drafted the position papers with input from me and the others.

We started the process by identifying what was wrong with

welfare. We came up with two overall flaws in the system. First, it did not encourage, and even discouraged, recipients from taking steps to become self-sufficient. It did not require people to do anything to receive their checks—they didn't have to work, they didn't have to go to school. All they had to do was qualify. And if people did some work, their benefits were reduced. It discouraged marriage. If a woman married the father of her child, in most cases she was ineligible for welfare. It encouraged young single women with children to set up their own households—if they stayed at home with their parents or grandparents they usually were not eligible for the same benefits. Once a young woman and her child were on their own and receiving welfare, the program paid her higher benefits with each additional illegitimate child she had. Teen mothers on welfare were dropping out of high school and sitting at home collecting their monthly checks. Children on welfare were growing up and going on welfare themselves. They were repeating the mistakes of their parents, dropping out of school and going nowhere.

Second, welfare had no effective component for actually helping people become self-sufficient. It didn't provide comprehensive education, training, or job-search assistance to help people gain the tools to succeed. It didn't help recipients make the transition from public assistance to the workforce. People who pulled themselves off welfare and into a job often found themselves worse off. They were without child care or health insurance. The welfare bureaucracy was good at handing out checks, but basic things like helping people find reliable transportation so they could get to a job on time were not part of the program. And there was little in place to track down fathers and get them to pay their child support. Welfare was about sending out checks. It was not about enforcing parental responsibility and helping collect child support so mothers and children could get off welfare.

I wanted to help people by making welfare more like the real world. In the real world, parents have to get up and go to work in the morning. There are timelines and deadlines. Children have to go to school. Working families don't get an automatic raise when they have additional children, so why should people on welfare? Wisconsin had always been generous with its welfare programs. It was part of our Progressive tradition. I wanted to continue to help people, but by redirecting our compassion. As long as welfare sheltered people from real-world responsibilities, I believed, it would never truly help them.

Pam Anderson, my campaign scheduler, had fixed instructions to pack in as many stops as possible. To win the election, I knew I had to meet a lot of people. Pam took her assignment seriously. Because I was getting up before dawn, I often took naps while John Tries drove. (He probably napped during my speeches.) But one day, when John and I were traveling between Ashland and Superior in the very northern part of the state, I couldn't stop thinking about what I would do about welfare if I actually won.

We started talking about what could be done to break the cycle of welfare dependency—kids growing up in welfare families, teenage girls getting pregnant and starting the cycle over again for another generation. John said that when he was a policeman in Milwaukee, one of the big problems was kids on welfare dropping out of school, hanging out, and getting into trouble. We talked about how important education had been to our own parents when we were growing up—dropping out of school just wasn't an option. I thought, What a waste of potential talent; why can't we keep these kids in school? If we really were going to change things, the children had to get their educations so they could make something of their lives. From this discussion, we came up with my first commonsense welfare reform: If parents wanted to receive a welfare check, they had to keep their kids in school. As we talked about it in the car we also thought of a straightforward name for it. We called it Learnfare.

That night I called Rick Chandler and asked him to discuss the idea with the task force and include it in our paper on welfare reform. Among other things, the issue paper proposed reducing Wisconsin's cash welfare grant by 5 percent and using the money to fund more work-related services for people on welfare. That was a novel idea at the time. When it came to welfare, Republicans were saying, "Cut, cut, cut," and Democrats were saying, "Spend, spend, spend." I was saying, "Cut, but invest." I also proposed more aggressive child support collection, and said I would make changes to "maximize individual and family responsibility." When we released the paper, my opponent basically ignored it. But I used the position paper out on the stump to talk to people about what I wanted to do. I could tell it made sense to them.

After I was elected, welfare reform became one of my first major initiatives. Both houses of the legislature were controlled by the Democrats, so I knew that it would be difficult for me to enact major changes. So when it came time to choose my cabinet, the first thing I did was appoint a prominent Democrat to head the state Department of Health and Social Services (DHSS). Tim Cullen was not just any Democrat—he was the majority leader of the state senate. People were shocked, and a lot of Republicans were mad at me.

It turned out to be one of the smartest moves I could have made. It went a long way toward neutralizing legislative opposition to my reform initiatives. With the former leader of the Democrat-controlled senate helping lead the legislative effort, the public debate was less about a Republican governor trying to bash people on welfare and more about making fundamental changes to a system that wasn't working. To be sure, I got bashed—and still do—by liberal Democrats and their allies, but I had taken away a key piece of their rhetorical arsenal.

The proposals from my campaign were the basis for a major welfare reform initiative I proposed in my first budget, two months after being elected. It called for the establishment of Learnfare statewide and a 5 percent reduction in welfare cash benefits. The cut in welfare benefits meant a savings in state spending of $15 million. Rather than pocket that money, I plowed all of it—plus $2.5 million more—into new or expanded services to help people get off welfare and stay off.

I proposed new funding to help people make the transition from welfare to work. This included child care benefits for up to nine months when recipients got off welfare and started working, and child care benefits for teen mothers on welfare so they could stay in school. I also increased funding for health care so more low-income families would be covered. I was trying to help more low-income working people avoid going on welfare and to extend coverage for people getting off welfare and starting work.

My 1987 budget also proposed a major expansion of a pilot project my Democrat predecessor had established before the election. It was called the Work Experience and Job Training (WEJT) program, and it provided job training for a limited number of welfare recipients. I thought it was a good idea, worthy of a major effort. So I increased funding for the program by 300 percent and expanded it into more counties.

I also beefed up our efforts to collect child support from parents—mostly fathers—who were not living in the home. It made absolutely no sense to me that we weren't doing more to hold people responsible for bringing a child into this world. Fathers were walking away from their responsibilities and leaving taxpayers the bill. The budget proposed a new link between the welfare office and the court system, which handled child support orders. It gave courts the authority to order non-custodial parents to participate in our expanded job-training program to gain employment skills so they could start working and pay their child support.

Despite the fact that I was redirecting funds to help people move off welfare, the Democrats in the legislature opposed my proposed cut in welfare benefits. It was cruel, they argued, even though the state's benefit level after the cut was still the ninth highest in the nation. Yet they didn't want to appear to be too "soft" on welfare recipients, so they reduced my cut to 1 percent. This made no sense to me. For political purposes, they were conceding that benefit levels should be cut, but the meager amount meant no funding for the new services I was proposing. It was a status quo solution. Welfare would be run the same way in Wisconsin, but recipients would have a little less money.

Learnfare generated a lot of controversy—no other state in the nation had tried it. When I first proposed my budget, I had wanted Learnfare to include all teens, but was persuaded by staff that this would be too much too soon. The Democrats would block it as too "radical." So my initial outline limited the program to teen mothers on welfare who had dropped out of school. The proposal was very simple. If a teen mother dropped out of school or did not attend regularly, her monthly welfare check would be reduced until she attended school regularly. Betty Jo Nelsen, the assembly minority leader, and other legislators convinced me to go further. Dropping out of school was a problem for all teens on welfare, including young men. If we wanted to start breaking the cycle of dependency, we had to do something dramatic to shake up the system. I broadened the proposal to include all families on welfare. If any teen between the ages of thirteen and nineteen dropped out, the family's monthly check would be reduced.

Wisconsin liberals were outraged. "What if the kids don't want to go to school?" they demanded. That made me think back to my own childhood. The notion of going downstairs in the morning as a youngster and announcing that I had decided not to go to school that day was incomprehensible. My father would've said, "Don't let the door hit you as you're flying through it." Learnfare to me is like the "tough love" I grew up with. I saw no reason that government could not or should not try to promote that same kind of tough love.

Two other complaints against Learnfare were: "Parents shouldn't be held responsible for the behavior of their children" and "It is unfair for one child's truancy to hurt the whole family by reducing the monthly check for everyone." The answer to the first complaint is, "Yes, parents should be held accountable for the behavior of their children." If taxpayers are paying to help needy families, then government has a duty to expect responsible behavior from the recipients in return for the aid.

The best response to the second complaint came later from a welfare mother who was trying everything she could to keep her children in school and out of trouble. In a newspaper interview, she said Learnfare was a valuable tool in her struggle because it gave her children a greater sense of responsibility, knowing that skipping school was not just an individual act, but something that had an impact on the whole family. Learnfare helped her demonstrate tangibly to her children what skipping school really meant. She detailed for her fourteen-year-old son the monthly expenses for rent, gas, food, electricity, all the way down to the $40 for his infant sister's diapers. Then the Milwaukee woman drove home the point. "I told him if he cuts school, I won't be able to buy him clothes at all, that he'd be wearing raggedy clothes, and people would laugh at him." That got his attention, the newspaper reported.

"Mean-spirited" and "racist," the liberal legislators said. Getting Learnfare passed by a Democrat legislature was going to be tough. I agreed to set up a special committee of Republican and Democrat legislative leaders, chaired by Tim Cullen, secretary of DHSS, to try to work out a compromise. The group included two strong Republican woman, assembly minority leader Betty Jo Nelsen from Milwaukee County and senate minority leader Susan Engeleiter, from Waukesha County. Their work kept Learnfare alive, and although the legislature pared it back to my original proposal, affecting teen parents only, it passed the legislature.

While all this was going on, we were busy on another front. We had to get waivers from Washington to try most of the things I was proposing. Washington's rules did not allow us to reduce benefits for poor school attendance. We couldn't require people to participate in job training, and we couldn't extend medical coverage to people while they were making the transition from welfare to work.

I also needed waivers to try another small but practical reform. Under federal rules, people who start working part-time while on welfare have their benefits cut. A recipient could "disregard" a small portion of earnings, but only for four months. After that, the earnings reduced the welfare check dollar for dollar. I wanted to give people twelve months so they could work longer before being penalized. Many people needed that work experience to become employable in a full-time job. It made sense to me, but I had to get permission from the federal government to do what was right for Wisconsin.

This was my first of many experiences with the waiver process. I thought it would be relatively easy. After all, I had just been elected governor by the people of my state. I had promised to change welfare, the people agreed with me, and now I was keeping my end of the bargain. Besides, this was the Reagan Administration, and the secretary of HHS, Otis "Doc" Bowen, was a former Republican governor of Indiana. A cakewalk, I thought.

What I underestimated was the power of unelected federal bureaucrats. They were the ones who could make or break you. It didn't hurt to have the president and the secretary on your side, but it didn't help that much either. The other major problem was that the federal government hadn't had much experience at the time granting welfare waivers to states. We were asking for a lot more than anyone had before, so the process was as new to them as it was to us. After several months of negotiation and some arm-twisting by the White House, we finally received permission to try the reforms in our state.

The state legislature, meanwhile, had passed the budget after reducing my proposed 5 percent cut in welfare benefits to 1 percent and limiting the scope of Learnfare to include only teen mothers. The question for me was, Should I use the governor's veto power to restore my original benefit cut and the broader Learnfare program?

The veto power of Wisconsin's governors, granted by the state constitution, is more extensive than that in any other state. It is a "partial" veto, which allows the governor to strike out individual words and digits as well as sentences and paragraphs from budget bills passed by the legislature. For example, the governor can strike a zero in a $40 million appropriation to make it $4 million. Or if the legislature has passed a bill saying, "The Department of Corrections will not incarcerate any more violent criminals," the governor can veto the words "not" and "any" to create an opposite result. The legislature can override the governor's vetoes with a two-thirds majority in each house.

I decided to restore the broader Learnfare proposal—to include all welfare families, not just those headed by teen mothers—but I was debating with my staff over whether I should use the veto to restore the 5 percent benefit cut. On the evening before the day I was to have all my budget vetoes completed, my staff met in the basement of the executive residence to go through the line items we hadn't resolved.

Tim Cullen, my DHSS secretary, was opposed to my "creative vetoing," largely on philosophical grounds. My senior aide and secretary of the Department of Administration, Jim Klauser, agreed with Cullen. The liberals would be able to paint me as harsh, he argued. We had gotten most of what we wanted in the budget. Conservative Republicans were pleased and the Democrats had not succeeded in making us look "extreme." Better to wait for another time, he counseled. Betty Jo Nelsen, on the other hand, argued strongly for the veto. We had the opportunity to move welfare in a new direction, and the benefit cut was essential to accomplishing that. The Democrats would be unable to generate enough support to override the veto, she predicted.

In the end, Betty Jo was right. I needed to take a gamble to really change things. I restored the benefit cut, and the legislature failed to override that or any of my 290 other vetoes in the budget. In fact, in an attempt to override my veto reducing the welfare benefit, only fourteen of nineteen Democrats in the senate voted with their leadership. The override attempt not only failed to achieve the necessary two-thirds of the votes, it failed even to gain a majority of votes. The fact that I had promised to put all the money into child care, health care, job training, child support collection, and other services for welfare recipients made all the difference in the world. To some Democrats and most of the public, we weren't slashing people's benefits, we were redirecting them to change welfare into a program that would help recipients become self-sufficient.

We had made it clear that our welfare reforms were experiments. We weren't sure how they would work until we tried them. People understood that, I think in large part because of Wisconsin's Progressive past—our history of innovative government. People wanted government to try new approaches, particularly with programs like welfare that clearly weren't working well. It made sense to most people that you have to try things out in the real world and modify them based on what you learn. Although government rarely seems able to acknowledge it, you don't usually get everything right the first time.

We learned that with Learnfare. We implemented it right away in 1988 in each of Wisconsin's seventy-two counties. It was a mistake to go statewide so soon. We underestimated two important realities. The first was the resistance to such a major change among welfare workers, particularly in Milwaukee County, where most welfare recipients lived. Wisconsin is one of a handful of states in which welfare programs are administered at the local level. Although all states have local welfare offices, most are staffed by state employees. In Wisconsin, the county welfare offices are run by county employees. The state provides the funding, establishes what the programs are, and contracts with counties to provide the services. Although the state has a supervisory role, the county welfare offices have a level of independence not found in most states. This decentralization of authority, again, is rooted in Wisconsin's turn-of-the-century Progressive movement. In the long run, it works well. It promotes flexibility and creativity—and even some healthy competition among counties to outperform one another. One county's approach to a particular problem may not work as well in another county, and vice versa.

As we started implementing Learnfare in 1988, though, it became clear that we were trying to achieve, in a very short time, a major change in the local welfare offices. We were asking them to perform a new job. They were used to processing applications and giving people money. We wanted them to track school attendance and take money away from recipients who were violating the new attendance requirements. The fact that they were not our employees made it even more difficult.

County officials in predominantly Democrat Milwaukee didn't like Learnfare and didn't want to do it. Even worse, we soon discovered that the Milwaukee public schools had no consistent method of tracking student attendance. It was a hodgepodge, and many schools simply had no idea who was there and who was not. (We found this very interesting. The state was paying school aid to Milwaukee on a per-pupil basis. The schools had never told us that some of the students we were paying for weren't actually there.) Suddenly, the welfare office needed to monitor attendance, and to do that, it had to rely on the school records. If a student whose family was receiving AFDC amassed ten unexcused absences in one semester, the student was placed on "monitor" status. Three subsequent unexcused absences in a month resulted in a "sanction"—a reduction in the monthly welfare check. Accurate attendance records were critical to the operation of Learnfare.

Almost immediately, a liberal interest group filed suit in federal court. It had found a welfare recipient who had been improperly sanctioned due to faulty attendance records. In this case, the attendance records provided to the welfare office did not match the records at the school. As a result of the court case, we had to hire people to double-check attendance records. Every month we had to verify that the information the welfare office received matched the attendance record at the school. Among other things, the court settlement required the addition of caseworkers and a more formal notice procedure to recipients before a sanction was applied.

Although I opposed it at the time because of the added costs, the court's ruling requiring caseworkers actually improved Learn-fare. Additional caseworkers have allowed us to help get children and families back on track and avoid benefit cuts for lack of school attendance. When a welfare child begins having atten-dance problems, a Learnfare caseworker is notified by the school district. The caseworker contacts the family, lets the family know that the benefit level could be reduced if there are more unex-cused absences, and helps address problems at home, like alcohol or drug abuse, that may be leading to the truancy. Caseworkers can now arrange treatment programs and counseling to help elim-inate those underlying problems. This person-to-person contact wasn't happening before Learnfare. No one was checking atten-dance and contacting the family when problems started. As one young woman told me about her experience on Learnfare, "The counselors got me back on track. I got enough motivation to go back to school and I got my GED [general equivalency diploma]."

We could tell from talking with the county offices that working directly with people to help solve their problems was more important than doing paperwork in the office. It made a difference in people's lives. One young woman was an eighteen-year-old dropout and parent. She had an abusive boyfriend. Annie Elam, a case manager in Racine County, sent her numer-ous letters offering help, but the boyfriend intercepted them. When the woman actually received one of the letters, she con-tacted Annie and they put together a plan. She dumped the boyfriend and earned her GED in five weeks. Another young woman was referred to Learnfare at age fifteen for excessive truancy. Through the persistence of her caseworker, she contacted a youth outreach worker who got her involved in a work program in a career she was interested in. The job showed her she needed an education to do what she really wanted, so she enrolled in an alternative education program. Her attendance was perfect and she earned an A average.

That is another thing we learned from operating Learnfare—often the most successful solution was alternative education options such as technical school programs or GED programs run by county welfare offices. So we increased funding for such programs as well as money for child care and transportation to and from day care for the children of teen mothers who needed to get their education.

We discovered while running the program that many of the teens in trouble had established poor attendance patterns in elementary school. Caseworkers reported that problems in the home were the biggest single factor in teens dropping out of high school—and these problems usually had been going on for years. So in 1994, we expanded Learnfare to include younger children, ages six through twelve. Instead of targeting simply the attendance records of these very young children, we put the emphasis on caseworkers identifying problems early and working with parents to try to solve them. Only if a family refuses to work with caseworkers will benefits be cut. Learning from our first experience, we also phased in the expansion rather than trying it all at once. We started in four pilot counties, and phased in the new age groups over a two-year period.

Learnfare's greatest benefit is something that is very difficult to measure. It has helped change people's attitudes. Word passed quickly among welfare recipients that the state would cut your benefits if you dropped out of school. This was acting as a deterrent—keeping people from dropping out when they may have before. But there is no empirical way to measure deterrence. Although the rate of sanctions under the program has fallen by 50 percent, and 97 percent of Learnfare students are attending school regularly, some studies show no significant difference in attendance compared to a control group that is not subject to Learnfare. Has Learnfare changed the welfare culture to such an extent that people in the control group are changing their behavior? We can't tell from the data, but we do know that more welfare recipients are staying in school.

To me, Learnfare is not a single, perfect solution, but an important element of an overall strategy to change the culture of welfare dependency. Shortly after we started the program, I received a letter from a young woman on welfare. She said she had thought I was the meanest person on earth. She had given birth to her first child when she was fifteen, her second when she was sixteen. Her mother and her grandmother had been on AFDC, and she figured that was her lot in life as well. But then Learnfare came along and her benefits were cut. She had to go back to school. She was writing to say that now she was hitting the books and getting A's. She was going to graduate from high school and go on to college. Her letter brought tears to my eyes. She had a whole new outlook on life and a whole new world of opportunities for herself and her children.

Periodically, I have invited welfare recipients to the governor's residence for lunch. It's my way of trying to solve problems the same way my father did in the grocery store in Elroy. At one lunch for Learnfare students, Marisa Mercado, a young woman who had dropped out of school but came back with the help of Learnfare, told me, "I didn't ever think before about going to college. Learnfare has really changed my mind about going to college." That new attitude also was expressed by Charles Grant, a young man who was skipping school and going nowhere. Learnfare put him back on track, helping him earn his GED. At a graduation ceremony for Learnfare students, Charles walked across the stage and was handed the diploma his hard work had earned. Afterward, he told a newspaper reporter, "I was so proud to walk across that stage, I wanted to do it six times. I wanted to do James Brown all over the place." To me, that is what welfare reform is all about.

After my first budget in 1987, we kept going with additional reforms. I knew we had an opportunity to do something dramatic, and I didn't want to lose the chance. During my campaign for governor, we had identified the ailments; now we needed to discover the cures. I decided the best approach was to try limited experiments that targeted specific problems with welfare. This small but very precise programming was politically achievable with a Democrat-controlled legislature. It was hard for them to block limited experiments because the public wanted change, and limited experiments seemed reasonable to most people. It also made common sense. Try reforms, see what works, and then expand what does and discard what doesn't.

One of the problems that everyone identified but no one was doing much about was the failure of fathers to take responsibility for the children they had helped bring into this world. When you think about it, welfare discriminates against women. It puts all the burden on them and does nothing to "make the daddies pay," as U.S. Senator Daniel Patrick Moynihan once described it. To me, both parents taking the responsibility for supporting their children is a bedrock moral issue. It also makes practical sense: the more we can enforce the responsibility of parents to pay their child support, the less likely it is that women and children will be on welfare.

I had talked about this issue during the 1986 campaign, and my 1987 budget had proposed increased collection efforts and a new link between welfare offices and the court system responsible for enforcing child support orders. These formed the foundation of Children First, a pilot project we started in two counties in 1990. The problem with child support collection efforts was that there was little the courts could do if the noncustodial parent—usually the father—claimed he had no job and no money. Children First changed that. Parents who weren't paying their child support were brought before the court and given two choices: pay the child support or go to jail. Almost always, the parent picked option number one, but then said, "Hey, I can't pay because I don't have a job." No problem. Children First helps the parent find work, or if unsuccessful, enrolls him in an unpaid community service job for sixteen weeks to gain the work experience necessary to get a job.

We tried the program in Fond du Lac and Racine counties, and were amazed at the results. The number of people paying child support increased by 83 percent and the amount paid went up by 237 percent. Faced with the prospect of sweeping streets or clearing ditches for four months, 77 percent of the parents suddenly came up with the money for child support. The program worked because of its simplicity. It was very straightforward, with no loopholes for people trying to dodge their responsibilities.

It also worked because the counties that ran it were enthusiastic about it. Learnfare had problems because counties didn't want to do it. I wasn't going to make that mistake again. So we let counties compete for Children First. We had enough money for two counties and we were only going to pick ones that really wanted it. The enthusiasm of the two counties selected made a difference when it came to putting the pieces together to make it work. The program relies on coordination among the welfare office, the judge, and the clerk of courts, which handles child support collections. All three components were on board and ready to go when we began the program.

As in most cases when you're trying something new, the success of Children First really came down to individual people who went out of their way to make it work. In Racine County, that person was Jerry Hamilton. Fathers who aren't paying their child support and don't have a job report to Jerry for job placement or community work experience. Jerry runs a good job-training program, but when it came to Children First, he went the extra mile. On his own, he raised private foundation money to start a fathers' club to complement Children First. To him, it wasn't just a matter of paying child support, it was getting the fathers to be part of the family, to accept the responsibility of helping raise their children. He says, "What we want is co-parenting. These kids need to know their fathers." Jerry is a towering man. He is warm and caring, but tough as nails on the fathers when he has to be. When the fathers come in the door, he tells them, "You're going to join the fathers' club and learn how to be a dad." They do.

In 1992, I went to Washington to ask permission to use our "waiver savings"—money we had saved the federal government by reducing our welfare rolls because of our reforms—to expand Children First into more Wisconsin counties. It was somewhat ironic. We had to ask permission in the first place to try reforms that were against their rules, and when they worked, we had to go back again to ask if we could use the savings to do more of what was working. In 1993, Washington said OK, we could use part of the savings to expand Children First to nine counties.

We again picked only counties that wanted to try the reform, but this time we had some problems. In some counties, the three agencies that needed to work together couldn't get along. Jean Rogers, who runs our welfare division, had to go to the counties and set up lunches with all the players and iron out their differences. This delayed the program in some counties, but within a few months, they were up and running. The results were impressive again. A 1994 study of the program in the nine counties found a 66 percent increase in the number of people paying child support and a 158 percent increase in the average payment. So in 1994, we added fourteen more counties and in 1996, we added nine others. With the later two expansions, however, we required counties to demonstrate that all the required agencies were ready and willing to work together before they could be selected.

The solid results of Children First, coupled with other initiatives to establish paternity and collect payments, helped Wisconsin increase child support collections by 134 percent since 1987. Welfare case closures due to child support collections grew by 22 percent from 1989 to 1993, saving nearly $67 million in welfare costs. At 37 percent, our child support collection rate is the second highest in the nation, but we still have a long way to go. Nationwide, only 18 percent of child support is collected. Children are owed more than $34 billion that isn't being paid. It is an American tragedy. Getting those parents to pay would go a long way toward reducing welfare dependency among women and children.

While Children First was beginning in the first two counties, we were putting together another experimental reform to address related problems of establishing paternity in welfare cases, discouraging single parenting, and encouraging women not to have additional illegitimate children. I wanted to do something to promote the responsibilities of both parents and to try to discourage young women from having more children while on welfare. From the data, we knew that single parenting was the major underlying reason people went on welfare, and having additional children while on welfare was making it harder for people to get off welfare. For many Wisconsin welfare recipients, the pattern started when they were young—50 percent of recipients had their first child when they were teenagers. As with Learnfare, I believed we had to focus on young people to change their behavior before they became locked into long-term dependency. We decided we needed a reform directed at single parents—both men and women—under the age of twenty.

Eloise Anderson, who ran our child welfare division of DHSS at the time, was the driving force behind developing an experiment that would discourage single parenting and encourage self-sufficiency among young people on welfare. Unfortunately, Governor Pete Wilson of California hired her away from me, and she's now running California's welfare programs. Eloise is African American. And partly because of that, she could speak out boldly about reforms that I would've been labeled "racist" for proposing. She had no tolerance for young fathers who shirked their responsibilities, young women who acted like helpless victims, or liberal do-gooders who she felt enabled that behavior. Like me, she believed strongly that any kind of work—flipping burgers at McDonald's—was better than non-work.

Eloise identified several "diseases" in the current welfare system that promoted single parenting and other irresponsible behavior, and she developed a broad reform package that would target those specific problems in a limited number of counties. She pointed out that welfare discourages marriage by making many young women ineligible for welfare if they marry the father of their children. (Welfare does this by denying benefits to a two-parent household if the parents have no work history.) Because many low-income teens don't have work experience, welfare encourages young mothers to set up their own households to be eligible for AFDC. So we put together a waiver request to get permission from Washington to eliminate these provisions.

We also discovered that there was little in the way of a comprehensive effort to establish paternity when a young woman applies for welfare. We couldn't get the fathers more involved in helping to support their children if we didn't know who they were. So we made paternity establishment a priority in the welfare application process for teen mothers under the pilot project. In cases where paternity is established and the parents live together, we made it a requirement that, to receive AFDC benefits, both parents had to participate in job training and other services such as classes in how to be good parent. And we included a Children First component that required noncustodial parents to pay their child support. All these were against Washington's rules, so we had to submit waivers to implement them.

Under federal law, states must pay higher welfare benefits for each additional child a mother has. In Wisconsin, the differ-

ence is $248 a month for one child and $617 for four children.
(The argument is that it takes more to support more children.)
Though the reasoning made sense, the regulations were perverse. If we wanted to encourage responsible parenting, I felt we
had to make welfare more like the real world. No one gets a
raise for having additional children. Having additional children
is an important decision that, among other things, affects the
family budget. Why should it be different for people who are on
welfare? In the name of "compassion," Washington and the
enlightened bureaucrats there have insulated people on welfare
from the real-world consequence of their individual actions. So,
again, we put together a waiver request asking the Bush
Administration to allow us to change the federal approach. We
asked for permission to cut in half the normal increase for
recipients who have one additional child while on welfare, and
provide no additional increases beyond that. (This was a compromise. I had wanted to establish one flat rate, regardless of
family size, but the legislature wouldn't allow it.)

The other major component we wanted to address was
work. Although Learnfare required the teens to stay in school,
we thought it was important to help them develop practical job
skills as well. Again, we identified specific provisions in welfare
that discourage work, and asked Washington if we could do
away with them. In 1987, the Reagan Administration had
granted our request to allow people on welfare to work for
twelve months before their earnings were fully counted against
their welfare benefits. We went back to Washington and asked
for no time limit at all. In addition, we asked the Bush Administration to increase the amount welfare recipients under this
experiment could earn before benefits would be reduced. Under
federal law, AFDC recipients are normally allowed to keep the
first $30 and one-third of all additional earnings each month
for a total of four months, and only $30 over the next eight
months. We wanted to allow them to keep the first $200 and
one-half of their earnings each month with no time limit.

When we had put all the pieces together, we called it the Parental and Family Responsibility (PFR) Demonstration Project. When I introduced it in the legislature, the Democrats immediately pounced, dubbing it "Bridefare." They characterized it as forcing young people to get married—state-sanctioned "shotgun weddings." The rhetoric seemed accurate, but it wasn't. The proposal removed disincentives toward marriage from the existing welfare system, but it didn't require anyone to get married. The "Bridefare" label stuck, however, which made it tougher to pass in the still Democrat-controlled legislature. Eloise Anderson, however, made the difference in getting it passed. She took on the Democrats in television interviews and in the newspapers and swung public sentiment our way. The Bush Administration approved our waivers, and the president and I announced the experiment in a ceremony at the White House.

We started PFR in four counties. We soon began to learn which of our assumptions had been right and which had been wrong. Removing the penalties for marriage had little effect on encouraging teen parents to marry. The decision to get married was based on more complicated factors than the presence or absence of welfare penalties. However, the program did have an impact on discouraging young women from having additional children. Preliminary data show that less than 10 percent of the teens in the program had another pregnancy, versus a national rate of 30 percent. From our aggressive efforts to establish paternity, we learned something shocking. Many of the fathers of these teen mothers' children were not teenage boys, but older men. A major focus of PFR was to help bring fathers back into the family, but when the father is thirty or forty years old and the mother is fifteen, the father belongs in jail.

Helping people move from welfare to work was the underlying component of all our reforms. Learnfare, Children First, and PFR all tied into our ongoing welfare-to-work reform on a broader level. The Wisconsin Education and Job Training program, which I expanded in 1987, became Workfare, and we expanded it to every county in the state. In 1988, the federal government established the Family Support Act, which created the Job Opportunities and Basic Skill (JOBS) program. JOBS was modeled after the Workfare program we were already running. It provided funds to states to set up job-training programs for welfare recipients, although it came with a new batch of federal rules and regulations, and it didn't require anyone on welfare to work. By 1991, Wisconsin was one of only six states to fully fund the JOBS program. We did this by spending the full amount of state dollars necessary to receive the maximum amount of federal matching funds for the program.

We experimented gradually with minor but significant changes in the JOBS program—changes we could make without having to ask permission from Washington. The way it was designed by federal officials, JOBS was a training program for welfare recipients more than a jobs program. Training is important, but working in an actual job is often the best training of all. Many people on welfare weren't used to getting up every morning, taking a shower, getting the kids fed and off to school or day care, and showing up for work. These were basic skills that could not be taught in a classroom. So we increased the number of people who were required to participate in actual work.

When we learned from county offices that many of the training programs seemed irrelevant, we pushed them to create training for actual jobs that existed in the community. This meant working more closely with local businesses, civic organizations, and chambers of commerce. I bolstered that effort by repeatedly asking businesses to hire people off welfare rolls, and many did—proving the real value of the bully pulpit.

We also began to integrate other state agencies and programs more closely with welfare. We plugged into our system of vocational and technical colleges to provide job-based skills training for welfare recipients. Working with the business community, our state Labor Department was establishing job centers throughout the state to link job openings with job seekers via computer. We began integrating that system into our welfare offices at the county level.

We were requiring more of welfare recipients, but we were also being more generous. I substantially increased funding for child care and gave counties more flexibility in moving money from other accounts into child care. We talked regularly with local welfare offices to review what they needed to help people get off welfare. They gave us practical suggestions like, "People don't have reliable transportation," or "They are penalized for earning money." So we again sought and received waivers from Washington to make commonsense changes. Along with two other states, we received permission from the Bush Administration to eliminate the "hundred-hour rule," a provision of the current welfare system that reduces welfare payments when one parent in a two-parent family works more than ninety-nine hours in a month. In addition, we raised the federally imposed limit on the value of the car welfare recipients could own. We also changed the federal rule allowing welfare recipients to have no more than $1,000 in assets before being penalized. We increased the limit to $10,000 provided that the funds were used for educational advancement and improving employability.

All these changes were practical reforms designed to improve recipients' ability to become independent. Rather than penalizing positive individual behavior like working and saving, we made changes that enabled people to realize the reward of such responsible actions. Commonsense changes. Helping recipients own a reliable car so they could get to work. Allowing them to save money for education for themselves and their children. Encouraging two parents to stay in the home by allowing one parent to work longer hours to support the family.

As we made these changes and observed how they were working in the field, it became clear that a mixture of requiring more from recipients and providing more assistance to help them become self-sufficient was working. One outside observer who has studied our success, Professor Lawrence M. Mead of Princeton University, describes it this way: "Wisconsin attempts to blend assistance to the poor with specific directions aimed at helping them avoid dependency. They help the needy, but they also confront adults with their responsibilities."

Professor Mead's study only reaffirmed what we were already observing and hearing from welfare workers and welfare recipients. Velma Grits, a mother of three who got off welfare with the help of Wisconsin's JOBS program, said that without a work requirement, "I'd probably still be in front of the TV. I'm grateful they did push." Brenda Brown, a former welfare recipient with two children, said she was "really mad—angry" when she was first told she had to start job training. But without that "nudge," she acknowledged, "I would still be on welfare. I wouldn't have gotten a job." Adds Susan Shiesl, a mother of two who found work through the JOBS program, "They pushed me into figuring out what I wanted to do with myself."

When I ran for reelection in 1990, continuing Wisconsin's welfare reforms was something I emphasized to voters. In the previous four years, 69,000 people had moved off Wisconsin's welfare rolls. My opponent, the speaker of the state assembly, criticized my reforms as "too harsh." That was the prevailing political posture of Democrats in Wisconsin and nationally during that time. They weren't interested in making major changes in the welfare system. They focused more on criticizing my reforms. I could tell the public had moved beyond that partisan rhetoric. They knew the system wasn't working and they wanted someone to change it. After I was reelected, I was excited about having four more years to try more reforms. We still had a long way to go.

REPLACING WELFARE WITH WORK

In 1992, I met with George Bush at the White House and told him about the changes taking place in Wisconsin. I was excited about the possibilities of welfare reform, and I encouraged him to talk more about welfare in his campaign. The president was interested, but when I pressed my case with former Secretary of State James Baker, who was running the campaign, I could see I was not connecting. It was astounding to me that the Bush campaign would allow Bill Clinton to "steal away" welfare reform.

As the campaign went along, it really started to irritate me. It seemed that whenever Bill Clinton saw his poll numbers go down, he would start talking about "ending welfare as we know it." I knew Bill Clinton. We had worked together at the National Governors' Association on the JOBS program that Congress passed as part of the Family Support Act of 1988. He had done some welfare reform in Arkansas, but nothing approaching what we had accomplished in Wisconsin. I knew his thinking on welfare, and I knew he would have trouble doing anything major to change the system. He was too beholden to the Children's Defense Fund and other liberal groups that wanted to keep the federal system intact.

After the election, I attended the National Governors' Association's annual meeting in Washington, where Bill Clinton spoke. He told the nation's governors that his plan to "end welfare as we know it" would give new flexibility and authority to the states. He pledged to allow states unprecedented freedom to experiment with bold new changes. I returned home determined to test that promise.

At my regular weekly breakfast meeting with my senior aides, I told Jerry Whitburn, my secretary of health and social services, that I wanted to "end welfare as we know it." Bill Clinton was saying it, but I wanted us to actually do it. We talked about what that would really mean. I said, "To me it means making welfare like real life—you have to work for your pay and you can't stay on welfare forever." Jerry had been my labor secretary and a businessman, and he shared my interest in jobs.

We were prepared for this moment. Since I had hired Jerry

as DHSS secretary in 1991, we had been working on building a team to help us take welfare reform to the next level. To head our planning shop in DHSS, we hired Shannon Christian from the U.S. Department of Labor, where she had worked under secretaries Ann McLaughlin, Elizabeth Dole, and Lynn Martin. From the growing Wisconsin Policy Research Institute in Milwaukee, we recruited a bright young analyst, John Wagner. We hired Jason Turner, who managed the AFDC and JOBS training programs for the Bush Administration. And from the West Coast, where the GAIN (welfare for work) program was getting national attention, we lured Steve Perales, one of the program's senior managers. (Perales hadn't expected to be entertained at a Governor's Residence reception on the day he came to Madison to interview, but he was, and we got him.) In addition, we had a staff at DHSS who had the invaluable experience of working in the field with the reforms we had implemented over the previous five years. This was a team other states didn't have, and it gave us unique tools to develop policy options.

We also wanted to expose our administration to all the ideas that were available on welfare and dependency. We invited Harvard's David Ellwood, author of *Poor Support* and later a key Clinton aide on welfare policy, to Madison and grilled him on child support ideas. Princeton's Lawrence Mead, author of *Beyond Entitlement* and *The New Politics of Poverty*, came several times. I had Mickey Kaus, author of *The End of Equality*, to breakfast at the Governor's Residence to discuss his ideas. LaDonna Pavetti of the Urban Institute briefed me on her research on people leaving welfare. Charles Murray, perhaps the nation's most provocative welfare reform thinker, came to Madison to discuss his ideas. We were ready to overhaul a program that hadn't worked well for decades, and we invested a lot of time in trying to get all information that was available.

Jerry assembled a team at DHSS to develop our proposal to "end welfare as we know it." Over a two-month period, a task force including Jerry and DHSS staffers Jean Rogers, Gail

Propsom, Mary Rowin, Jean Sheil, Shannon Christian, and Gene Kussart worked on the plan. They started by asking the question, "If we could create a replacement to welfare, what would it look like?" They came up with answers like these: We would pay people for the number of hours they work, the business community would be an active partner in helping people find jobs, and we would provide child care and health care while people make the transition from welfare to work. Many of the ideas were elements of reforms we were already trying. This was an opportunity to put them together. It was an opportunity to change the culture of welfare dependency.

During periodic briefings on their progress, I realized that the group disagreed over how long benefits should last. Some wanted a two-year time limit; others thought that was too harsh. "What if people can't find private sector jobs within two years?" they asked. When the proposal was nearly finished and Jean Rogers was briefing me on its contents, she again raised the issue of time limits. I jumped on it. This reform had to be about changing the fundamental culture of welfare. To do that, there had to be a ticking clock. Time limits were a must. Both welfare recipients and welfare workers needed to know that when recipients walked in the door, there was a certain date when they had to be off welfare and into a job. Without it, people's natural tendency to procrastinate would set in. There was no answer to the question "what if" people can't find work after two years. I was confident we could find jobs for everyone who wanted to work, but I couldn't prove it. On the other hand, I was certain that if we did not have a time limit, we would never know if it could be done.

I announced the proposal in May 1993, even before we had received waivers from the Clinton Administration to do it. We called the reform Work Not Welfare, and it was the nation's first welfare reform to require work and place a limit on how long an individual can receive welfare benefits. It proposed the most comprehensive approach to welfare reform we, or anyone, had tried. It replaced welfare as we know it with a program of temporary cash assistance; intensive job training and job placement; and child care, health care, and transportation assistance to help recipients make the transition to work and self-sufficiency.

Under Work Not Welfare, every individual applying for AFDC benefits signs a contract pledging to work in exchange for benefits. Within thirty days, recipients begin work in a private sector or public job, or begin training for a job. Cash benefits are paid based on the number of hours each recipient works or participates in training for work. After twelve months, the participant must be working in a private sector job for pay or in a public job in exchange for benefits. Child care is provided to those who need it. After twenty-four months, cash benefits end, but transitional benefits—child care and health care—continue for twelve months for those who leave welfare for work. The state guarantees access to job training and education, and a team of employment specialists is assigned to each participant to help him or her get a job. A Community Steering Committee comprising local businesses, community organizations, and county government helps link participants to jobs in the community.

Shortly after I announced Work Not Welfare in June 1993, Bill Clinton announced his proposal to end welfare. It differed substantially from ours. Under Work Not Welfare, recipients must begin work or training for work within thirty days. The Clinton plan allowed recipients to receive cash benefits for two years before participating in work or training for work. Work Not Welfare established a two-year time limit for people to be on welfare, and did not provide public jobs after the two-year time limit expired. The Clinton proposal allowed people to stay on welfare indefinitely. After two years, recipients were required to participate in public works jobs, but there was no time limit on the government-funded jobs.

Clinton's proposal didn't really change welfare. It died in Congress, while Work Not Welfare was approved by the

Wisconsin legislature. Before passage, liberals in the state legislature tried to add a provision guaranteeing government-funded jobs after the two-year time limit. To my thinking, this would have eviscerated the experiment. With a guaranteed job at the end of the road, the urgency of preparing for and finding a job would be lost. I wanted to determine how quickly we could move people from welfare to work—how substantially we could change the culture of welfare. Guaranteed jobs were part of the old dependency culture.

Getting waivers from the Clinton Administration to try Work Not Welfare was an interesting endeavor. On one hand, we were helping the Democrat president by allowing him to show that he was willing to let a state end welfare as we know it. He must have known he would take a lot of criticism in the press for blocking what he had promised to do during the campaign. On the other hand, the administration was being lobbied by liberal groups not to let us go too far.

A team of six people at DHSS spent thousands of hours over a ninety-day period preparing, modifying, and negotiating the waivers. We had to get exemptions from forty-nine separate federal rules and regulations. Federal rules prohibited us from tying benefits to work—we couldn't pay cash benefits based on the number of hours people worked. Washington's regulations also forbid states from placing time limits on how long someone can be on welfare. As with any waiver request, we had to describe what we wanted to do, why we wanted to do it, and what federal rules and regulations the reform would impact, and we had to design a system for measuring what the reform achieved.

Federal bureaucrats wanted us to use an evaluation process that relied on a randomly selected control group. This was the standard academically prescribed method for testing such experiments. It required setting up a control group of welfare recipients who would not have to comply with Work Not Welfare, and later measuring the differences between the control group and those who had to comply with the program. We didn't want to do it that way. Work Not Welfare was based on the premise that we could change the whole culture of welfare. Businesses, schools, volunteers, and social services would work together to help an AFDC parent find and hold a job. How could the members of the control group be kept "pure" from the changes going on around them? We had already faced the same problem with Learnfare, where we couldn't determine whether the school attendance patterns of the control group were being influenced by the wide-scale perception that school attendance was required of welfare recipients.

We wanted to try a "pre-post" model, in which the outcomes of the reform would be measured by comparing what was happening before the reform to what was happening after it was in operation. This became a political battle, with liberal groups like the Center for Law and Social Policy pressuring the Clinton Administration not to allow it. We insisted, arguing that a "pre-post" evaluation model would be the only effective way of measuring the attitudinal shift brought about by the reform, which we considered central to the reform. How could we tell a business in the community that we wanted it to work aggressively to help welfare recipients and hire them, but only those recipients who were not in the federal government's control group? The randomly-selected-control-group method may have been favored by academics and welfare rights groups, but it didn't make any sense in the real world. After weeks of conference calls, faxes, and arguments, we prevailed. The evaluation section at HHS was going to allow us to be the first state to try this commonsense evaluation method.

Meanwhile, Jerry and Jean Rogers had traveled to Washington to negotiate the "larger issues" raised by our reform. They met with two assistant secretaries of HHS, senior Medicaid officials, and a top-ranking official at the U.S. Department of Agriculture, which is responsible for the food-stamp program. It wasn't pleasant. The people in Washington were not interested in a tight two-years-and-you're-off-welfare model. I had instructed Jerry and Jean not to compromise on this principle.

Weeks passed and I continued to press the Clinton Administration for waivers consistent with our legislation. Then HHS assistant secretary Mary Jo Bane called. She was prepared to fly out to Madison. She brought with her a federal team, and they spent a whole day with Jerry and his staff, negotiating the waivers. We took a hard line, and when they came over to my office at the end of the day, before catching their plane back to Washington, we had a clean time limit—two years and off. We were the only state in the nation with Washington's permission to try a no-nonsense time-limited reform.

Why did the Clinton Administration do it? It had no choice. Wisconsin was widely recognized as the national leader in welfare reform, so Bill Clinton could not afford *not* to do it. He had promised a bill to end welfare in his first hundred days in office, and now, two and a half years later, he hadn't done it. Bill Clinton was tardy, and Wisconsin was there to fill the void.

As with other reforms, we only selected counties that asked to try it. Although Milwaukee County, the county with the highest percentage of welfare recipients, didn't want to do it, fifteen other counties put on a full-court press to be chosen. County boards passed resolutions asking to be chosen. County leaders issued press releases in the local papers and asked their legislators in Madison to lobby me to select them. We received a steady stream of letters and phone calls from local businesses pledging to hire the people in the program. Local politicians, welfare workers, community organizations, and the chambers of commerce all got into the act. People had never seen the end of welfare—and they wanted to be a part of it.

We selected Pierce County, which is predominantly rural, and Fond du Lac County, which is more urban. I flew to the two counties in April and held press conferences announcing their selection. Eight months later—before the program had even begun—welfare rolls had dropped by 16 percent in the two counties. People knew reform was coming—so they were already going to work.

We started the program on January 1, 1995, and after fifteen months, welfare rolls declined by 44 percent in Fond du Lac County and 50 percent in Pierce County. From observing the reform in action, we learned that an immediate work requirement and a strict time limit worked better than job training and no deadlines. Rachel Ritacco, a mother of two, landed a private sector job after she was required to work for her benefits under the Work Not Welfare reform. She credited the program with giving her the motivation she lacked. "I was just tired of being on [welfare]. But I didn't have a good reason or push to get off it." Cathy Irizarri also got off welfare through the Work Not Welfare program. "There are too many people on welfare who are not even trying," she said. "It's not lack of opportunity, there is plenty of opportunity. It's lack of discipline on their part."

We had proven that we could reform the system, but had we changed the culture? From day one, we observed a much different focus in the welfare offices. Staff members were working more closely with recipients, and calling businesses, looking for jobs to help people become self-sufficient. The offices were humming. Back in 1993, when Jerry Whitburn and his staff were figuring out how to implement Work Not Welfare, there were questions about how local caseworkers should explain the two-year limit to welfare applicants. The team decided workers should tell people to think of it like a savings account—it is there when you need it, but it is a limited amount, so you shouldn't use it unless you have to. This prompted Jason Turner to ask an even more fundamental question. "Exactly what are we telling welfare applicants when they first walk in the door? What would happen," Jason asked, "if instead of filling out a welfare application right away, the welfare office spent time working with each person to see if they could get help *without going on welfare?*"

Common sense suggests that the best way to avoid becoming dependent is to not go on welfare in the first place.

So we started talking with each of the seventy-two county welfare offices to find out what they were doing when applicants first walked in the door. It was universal—applicants were handed an application to see if they qualified for AFDC.

We decided to change that. We knew from caseworkers and people on welfare that sometimes recipients needed only temporary help, but were sucked into the system once the checks started coming. During a lunch I hosted for welfare recipients at the Governor's Residence, one woman told me she landed on welfare for two years when her car broke down and she couldn't get to work. Surely we could help people with such problems without putting them on welfare. Like other government programs, welfare was too obsessed with uniformity. To every applicant we offered the same set of rigidly prescribed services—we said, "Fill in the application, here is what the program offers." It wasn't flexible enough to handle real-world problems. People have different needs and come to the welfare office from many different circumstances. Some people turn to welfare after a divorce or some other event that has put them in temporary distress. Helping pay a month's rent or arrange transportation to work may be what they need instead of a welfare check. Instead of giving people a form to fill out, wouldn't it make more sense to say, "Tell me your problem and let's see how we can help solve it."

We turned this commonsense concept into a reform called Work First and received approval from the legislature to try it in eighteen counties. We were able to start it in 1994, before Work Not Welfare, because we didn't need permission from Washington to try it. Under federal welfare rules, a state cannot *require* someone to talk to a caseworker about alternatives to welfare before filling out the application. We debated whether to go to Washington and ask for that authority, but instead we decided to try it first without any real enforcement mechanism. County welfare workers could talk to applicants about alternatives before they filled out the applications. If the applicant said,

"The heck with you, give me the application," Washington's rule said our workers had to comply.

The key to Work First was changing the job description of welfare workers. This process had already started with our JOBS program and other reforms that required workers to spend more time helping people become self-sufficient rather than simply processing applications and mailing checks. With Work First, we institutionalized and expanded it. Welfare office staff, once "income maintenance specialists," became "financial planners" and "resource specialists." Their job is to work with each applicant to find out what the applicant needs, and then to explore available options and resources that do not require going on welfare: alternatives such as nongovernment assistance, financial planning, and specific jobs available in the community. If an applicant still needs cash benefits, job search activities are begun as a first course, before people become complacent about not working.

This basic change in our approach to helping people had remarkable results. During the first eighteen months, 55 percent of the people who inquired about AFDC assistance found alternative resources to welfare. Welfare caseloads fell an average of 31 percent in the eighteen counties, and four of the counties reduced their welfare rolls by more than 50 percent. It taught us we could keep people off welfare by actively helping them find alternatives, and, for others, we could dramatically shorten their stay on welfare by beginning job placement efforts immediately. So, throughout 1995, we expanded Work First to forty-eight counties, and in January 1996, we expanded it statewide under the name Self-Sufficiency First. And because we had demonstrated success, we received permission from Washington to require it as a first step for all individuals seeking AFDC. Now if an applicant says, "The heck with you, give me the application," we can say, "There's the door."

By focusing on alternatives to welfare, the welfare office became a different place. Sue Meyers leads a team of financial planners and resource specialists in the Racine County welfare office. For ten years, she had worked in the same welfare office as an "income maintenance" worker. She and her staff now wonder why they weren't allowed to do this a long time ago. "In the past," she said, "it wasn't our place to discuss anything personal. Now we can talk about the resources and turn the tables on the clients. Rather than it being a question of what the government can do for them, it is now a question of what are they going to do for themselves." Many of her clients are in families that have been on welfare for years. For the first time in their lives, they are learning about other resources in their own communities and alternatives to welfare. Alesha Filiatrault, a welfare worker in Grant County, told my staff, "It doubled our workload to deal with options in addition to all the economic support rules. But working with people is more important than working with programs. In my mind, it just made perfect sense. This is the way you deal with human beings who are in crisis."

In a profile of Wisconsin welfare reforms for ABC News, reporter Rebecca Chase interviewed a woman who had moved to Wisconsin from Missouri. She went to the county welfare office and expected to fill out some forms and get a check as she had done before. Instead, she was met by a financial planner who set up two job interviews for her on the spot. She couldn't believe how different it was from the welfare offices she was used to. This is what changing the culture of welfare dependency is all about.

THE END OF WELFARE—PERIOD

In late 1993, as I approached another election, Wisconsin welfare rolls had declined more than those of any other state—down by 19 percent since we first started the reforms in 1987. During the same period, welfare rolls had shot up by 30 percent nationally. We had dropped from the eighth highest state in the nation in percentage of people on welfare to thirty-first. This was too much for Democrats in the state legislature. Although several conservative Democrats had supported many of my reforms, the official posture of the more liberal Democrat leaders had been to criticize and try to block or dismantle many of them. They were beginning to understand that they were on the wrong end of the issue. Welfare reform was working in Wisconsin, and the people supported it.

Walter Kunicki, the Democrat speaker of the assembly, was thinking about running against me in 1994. He had seen Bill Clinton take the issue away from Republicans on the national level, and he wanted to pull a fast one on me. Kunicki said we had tried a lot of pilot projects here and there, but Governor Thompson was really just tinkering around the edges. If the governor were really serious about welfare reform, Kunicki said, he would support legislation to end it completely. Kunicki proposed abolishing welfare completely in Wisconsin. He didn't propose an alternative, he just said we should abolish it by 1999. It was hollow, just like Bill Clinton's promise to "end welfare as we know it."

Even so, it was a bold political strategy. Replacing the entire AFDC system and coming up with a completely new alternative to welfare would be a huge task. It was a radical idea, and he was convinced I would veto it, which would hand the Democrats bragging rights on welfare reform in the next election.

Jerry Whitburn, whose leadership had helped guide us to the next level of reform over the past three years, was skeptical. This was a blatantly political move by the Democrats, and it should be vetoed. Maybe he was right. As the secretary of the department that would have to do most of the work, he knew what he was talking about. But I couldn't stop thinking, "This is a golden opportunity. How can the Democrats be so dumb to give me this chance to completely replace welfare?"

The bill passed both houses of the legislature, with the final vote occurring late on a Tuesday night. At seven-thirty the next morning, my senior staff met for our regular breakfast meeting. Jerry remained cool to the idea. I put down my fork and said, "Jerry, I'm going to sign it." And I later raised the ante—we moved up the timetable to end welfare by 1997.

The Democrats never even scored the political points they were after. I won the election in 1994, and for the first time since I had come to office, Republicans won both houses of the state legislature.

Despite his earlier reservations, Jerry enthusiastically threw himself into the project. He immediately put together a team of experts in DHSS to design the replacement—as we had done with Work Not Welfare. After eight years of implementing reforms, this was a group of people who knew more about changing welfare than anyone in the nation. He put together a bipartisan group of legislative leaders and a group of business and community-based leaders to work with us on the project.

We also enlisted the help of the Hudson Institute, a respected national think tank based in Indianapolis. In 1994, I met with Hudson Institute president Les Lenkowsky to discuss my goals for the alternative to welfare. I said I wanted a program built around work. I wanted to end the cash benefit premise of welfare and replace it with a real-world concept: pay for performance. Everyone would have to work, and only work would pay. I described it as a new contract in which government and low-income families have concomitant responsibilities. Government would agree to provide child care, health care, and other assistance for a limited time to help people find and keep a job. In return, people must be willing to take personal responsibility for themselves and their families. They have to get up in the morning, get the kids fed and off to school or day care, and get themselves to a job, just like ordinary hard-working Americans.

Lenkowsky assigned a full-time staff person, Andy Bush, to work on the Wisconsin project. Andy moved to Madison and spent a year helping us put together our alternative to welfare. He worked with Jean Rogers, Jason Turner, Jay Hein, and others on our staff to gather and analyze all relevant social service data and study the effectiveness of existing welfare programs in Wisconsin and across the nation. Hudson then prepared a series of policy options for us to consider.

In early 1995, Massachusetts Governor William Weld hired Jerry Whitburn away from me. Before he left to run Massachusetts's welfare programs, Jerry presented me with a name that Jim Malone of DHSS had come up with for the program we were developing to replace welfare. It was W2—Wisconsin Works. We were going to replace the welfare check with a paycheck—something we had talked about when I first hired him as DHSS secretary in 1991.

No other state was in a position to do this. No other state had comparable experience in the field, experimenting, discovering what works. In many ways, all we had to do was put the pieces together. Washington was fighting over whether it should give states the authority to run welfare, Clinton had vetoed the welfare reform bill passed by the new Republican Congress, but we were moving ahead without them. Really, the building blocks for W2 were what our laboratory of ideas had discovered over the past eight years. From the WEJT program I had expanded in 1987, we learned that people move faster when you require them to do something, either training or work. From the JOBS program that grew out of WEJT, we learned that the transition to work was faster still when you add an actual work requirement instead of just training. From Work First, we learned that many people don't even need the first welfare check when you help them look at other options as soon as they come in to apply. And from Work Not Welfare, we learned that people achieve self-sufficiency fastest when you combine an immediate work requirement with a time limit, which instills a sense of urgency, and encourages saving that government check for when they really need it.

We decided that W2 should focus on moving people into private sector jobs as soon as possible. That meant an immediate full-time work requirement and time limits, but it also meant community-based partnerships with private employers. So we expanded the model we had set up in Work Not Welfare to create Community Steering Committees comprising local businesses, charities, and civic groups to coordinate job placement for people. And since W2 would be a jobs program rather than a cash benefit program, we decided to eliminate our welfare department and shift responsibility for W2 to our new jobs department. Building on lessons from Work First and Work Not Welfare, we replaced "economic support" workers with financial planners and employment specialists. Welfare workers who had been spending 80 percent of their time doing paperwork would now spend 90 percent of their time working directly with people who need help.

We also knew that W2 would cost more money up front. The welfare reforms we had implemented since 1987 had reduced Wisconsin welfare rolls by 36 percent. As a result, taxpayers were saving $19 million each and every month. Our reforms have saved the state and federal government nearly $1 billion since 1987. Yet to achieve those savings, I had invested more money on the front end. To help people make the transition from welfare to work, we invested more money in child care, health care, transportation, and caseworkers who would work with people one-on-one. Child care expenditures alone increased by more than 300 percent, from $13 million in 1987 to $56 million in 1995. If W2 would require everyone to work immediately, we were going to have to expand child care funding even more substantially. And we knew from our other experiments that providing up to twelve months of child care and health insurance after people had left welfare to work helped them get off welfare and stay off. That would mean even more money. Yet I wanted to make W2 as close to the real world as possible, so we developed a provision that would require W2 participants to co-pay for these benefits as they began earning money.

As we began to develop a concrete, comprehensive replacement to welfare that reflected the lessons we had learned from welfare reform, we confronted an issue that dooms many government programs. How could we construct a program that achieves what we believe will work without making it so rigid that it cannot adjust to the realities of helping people with different needs and abilities? The last thing I wanted to do was replace one bureaucracy with another. We wanted to place people in private sector jobs, but we knew that some individuals would not be able to be placed in private sector jobs right away. There was no model in place to base this on—we had to use the experience we had gained over the previous eight years.

We decided that we needed to create different levels of jobs—levels that would reflect the "readiness levels" most people fit into when they showed up at the welfare office. At the same time, however, I didn't want to create a make-work program of government-funded jobs. It was essential to me that we build in incentives for people to move up the ladder to private employment as soon as possible. So we created three levels of subsidized employment. The lowest level paid the least, the next level paid more, and the final level paid the most, but none of them paid as much as a private sector job.

To further encourage people to move up the ladder and into unsubsidized jobs in the private sector, we limited the amount of time anyone could be in a subsidized job. Again, we put two-year time limits on each category of subsidized jobs, although an individual cannot spend two years in each of the three levels. We established an overall limit of five years on a person's eligibility for W2. Individuals can use the five years of help all at once or pieces at a time when they need it, but after using a total of five years of services, they are no longer eligible for assistance. This is a combination of the "ticking clock" and "savings account" approach we had tried with Work Not Welfare.

Our premise in establishing job levels for W2 was that everyone is capable of performing some kind of work. The highest level of subsidized employment we called trial jobs. After private sector jobs, this is the level we would require most recipients to start with, based on our experience running the statewide JOBS program and other reforms. Trial jobs are for people who have good attitudes toward work but aren't immediately employable, usually because they have very little experience holding down a job. W2 will place them in a private sector job and provide a subsidy to the employer. When they gain enough work experience, W2 will help them find an unsubsidized job, with the same employer if possible.

The middle rung of the job ladder is community service jobs. These are for a limited number of people whose poor work habits and skills make them unemployable with a private firm, even with a subsidy. They will be provided government-funded jobs in the community to gain basic work skills. The lowest level is transitional jobs, for people who have serious impediments to work. In addition to work, transitional jobs include services such as vocational rehabilitation and drug and alcohol treatment, to further prepare participants for work.

In addition to the work requirements, we incorporated elements of earlier reforms that had worked. We incorporated school attendance requirements from Learnfare, child support enforcement from Children First, and parental and family responsibility provisions—such as no additional pay for having more children—from PFR. After more than a year of work putting the program together, I introduced it to the now-Republican controlled state legislature in 1995. On April 25, 1996, I signed W2 into law. We are ready to implement this alternative to welfare in 1998, but there is one roadblock. We need permission from Washington to end welfare as we know it in Wisconsin. Yet again, we have to kiss the ring of Washington to accomplish what we know needs to be done in our state.

Although Bill Clinton has vetoed congressional attempts to

return authority over welfare to the states, such a change is all but inevitable. Americans will not tolerate much longer a welfare system that has lost its moral foundation. The lessons of Wisconsin welfare reform teach us that Washington really doesn't know best. We were able to achieve success only by removing ourselves from key components of the welfare system Washington imposes on Americans. Based on what I've learned, it makes no sense for Washington to dictate what welfare reforms the citizens of a state decide to undertake in their own communities. Why does there need to be another layer of government involved?

And yet, on May 4, 1996, Bill Clinton announced a typical Washington welfare reform. The federal government will require states to set up programs like Learnfare. In 1987, Wisconsin was the first state to do so, and now twenty-six states tie school attendance to welfare benefits. But why should Washington force states to do it? The Learnfare version Bill Clinton wants to impose on the states is based on a program in Ohio called LEAP, which was modeled after our Learnfare program, with an important difference: It pays welfare recipients more money if their children go to school. We already had a debate on that issue in Wisconsin and decided not to do it that way. Children are required by law to attend school. I see no reason government should pay them extra for doing it. This is just another way in which Washington's approach to welfare undermines individuals on welfare from taking personal responsibility for their actions. No matter what they say in Washington, in their view, welfare should not be like the real world.

In his weekly national radio address on May 18, 1996, Bill Clinton endorsed our W2 reform, calling it "a solid, bold welfare reform plan." Clinton's praise for the reform came three days before Senator Bob Dole was to visit Wisconsin and announce his support for W2. Although it was a shrewd political move, Bill Clinton's words have not been matched by his actions—something that has happened far too often with this president. Two days after the radio address, the White House began issuing qualifiers about the president's apparent endorsement, and an HHS official later told a congressional committee that the administration would not grant the necessary waivers for Wisconsin to implement the reform. This equivocation led *New York Times* reporter Robert Pear to write, "The administration's second thoughts are the latest shift in its course on welfare policy." The president who promised to end welfare as we know it has flip-flopped when presented with concrete efforts to do it.

On May 30, I delivered to the White House a 693-page application for the eighty-eight federal waivers we need to try W2. Fed up with the Clinton Administration's mixed signals on the issue, two Wisconsin congressmen, Representative Scott Klug and Representative Mark Neumann, introduced legislation in Congress to approve the waivers without waiting for the blessing of Washington's bureaucracy. On June 6, the House passed the legislation 289–136, although the measure has little chance of moving through the Senate. During the House floor debate over whether Wisconsin should have the freedom to try its own reforms, one Democrat from Tennessee succinctly expressed the one-size-fits-all mentality that still dominates much of Washington. "If we are going to spend time on the floor discussing welfare, we ought to be discussing a national welfare bill," said Representative John Tanner.*

Wisconsin has reduced its welfare rolls by 39 percent since 1987, far more than has any other state. We have achieved this by decoupling ourselves from Washington, not by following its mandates. We set broad policies at the state level but empowered local officials in the state's seventy-two counties to administer the programs. This decentralization encouraged flexibility

---

*As of this writing, Wisconsin's W2 waivers have not been approved by the Clinton Administration. On June 18, Bill Clinton told 6,000 nurses at the American Nurses Association convention in Washington that he planned to approve W2. Wisconsin will hold him to that promise.

and creativity among welfare offices seeking to help people achieve self-sufficiency. This essential flexibility is unachievable when Washington calls the shots. Wisconsin's success in reducing welfare rolls demonstrates that returning power from Washington to the states can result in government that is responsive, innovative, and effective at solving real-world problems—just as the authors of the Tenth Amendment envisioned.

Through the consistent elevation of welfare reform in the public debate and matching our rhetoric with concrete changes, the welfare climate in Wisconsin has changed. After nearly a decade of well-publicized reforms, welfare applicants in Wisconsin know they cannot expect something for nothing. And welfare workers know their job is not to hand out checks, but to help people find work. This new attitude has displaced the debilitating culture of dependency that permeates much of the welfare system in America today. In its place is an environment of hope and opportunity, shared responsibility, and the true compassion of a hand up to people who need help.

When we were working to put together W2, I received a letter from a former welfare recipient who had attended a lunch I hosted for welfare recipients at the Governor's Residence two years earlier. She was getting a promotion at work, but it required her to move to Arizona. She was writing to invite me to lunch should I ever be in Phoenix. And this time, she's buying.

CHAPTER FOUR

REDEFINING PUBLIC EDUCATION

Public education has come a long way since my parents taught in a two-room schoolhouse in Elroy. Technology has opened new doors to learning. Computers are now as common as blackboards in many elementary schools. Through fiber optics, schools are engaging in long-distance learning. Students in a rural school today can take courses in Japanese or advanced mathematics broadcast from another school district or another state. Educational opportunities are no longer limited to the boundaries of the classroom.

The two-room schoolhouse in Elroy is gone, replaced by a larger "consolidated" school with children from surrounding communities. Educating children is no longer a mom-and-pop operation. It is a big business. In Wisconsin, government spends $6 billion each year on K–12 schools. Funding for public schools is the largest expenditure in our state budget, and it has increased at a rate much greater than other government spending.

As early as the nineteenth century, Wisconsin was regarded as a progressive leader in education. Our first public school opened in the fall of 1836, one month before the territorial legislature's first meeting, and twelve years before Wisconsin even became a state. In 1845, the legislature passed a law allowing one community to experiment with free schools. It was not until 1865, twenty years after Wisconsin experimented with the concept, that public schools were common in other states across the nation. In the early years before bureaucracies were interested in governing public schools, communities voluntarily and informally supported their own schools. There were no school districts, no departments of education, and no formal means of taxation. If members of a community felt the desire to build a schoolhouse and educate their children, they made it happen. As historian Lloyd P. Jorgenson noted in his book *The Founding of Public Education in America,* "The most striking fact about early education in Wisconsin is that the movement for free schools was essentially a local one. Tax-supported schools were not created by territorial legislation; it would be closer to the truth to say that they developed in spite of such legislation."

Government's increased role in education has come about much in the same way it has expanded in other areas. The need for uniformity has resulted in more regulations, more centralized control, and more administrators. In 1848, Wisconsin established a state Department of Public Instruction (DPI) to ensure uniformity in public education. It is an "independent" agency that is not part of the governor's cabinet. (In 1996, I proposed and the legislature adopted a law to make DPI part of the governor's cabinet, but on a 7–0 vote, the state supreme court overturned that law.) The state superintendent of public instruction, who runs DPI, is elected in a statewide election, and is independent of the governor. Though it may be independent of the governor, in reality DPI is dominated by the education establishment. Politicians come and go but organized interests like the teachers union stay on forever, it seems. After a while, they have more influence over the bureaucracy, particularly when the governor can't appoint the head of the department. With an annual operating budget of $43 million and 625 employees, the agency creates and enforces hundreds of regulations on local schools. In 1980, the federal government added another layer with its own Department of Education.

As the education establishment of government bureaucracy and interest groups grew in size and power, their interests soon came into conflict with any significant change in the status quo. When I proposed reforms, they labeled not just my ideas but me as "anti-education," "anti-teacher," and, above all, "anti-children." Some of their characterizations—and purported facts about what I was trying to do or had done—were so absurd they would have been laughable if so many teachers-union members had not believed them. During my reelection campaigns, many would refuse to accept my literature. They would look at my young volunteers and shout, "I'm a teacher!" As though that were enough reason not to even read what I had to say. It was a sad irony. My wife is a public school teacher—she teaches sixth grade in the new Elroy-Kendall school. Both my parents were public school teachers. My grandfather George Thompson was a public school teacher. I was trying to improve education. I had some new ideas, but these people were conditioned not to even listen.

School spending started to climb at rates far outpacing inflation or enrollment increases. Meanwhile, educational achievement levels stayed the same—and in some places in the state, went down. When I was elected governor in 1986, property taxpayers—the people who pay for rising school spending—were up in arms. People were starting to wonder where all that money was going. There was a growing understanding on the campaign trail—in the coffee shops and the bowling alleys—that we weren't getting that much for our money.

One public school teacher asked in the 1991 book *The Exhausted School*, "How on earth did we ever accept the idea a government had the right to tell us where to go to school?" It's a good question. Government's monopoly on K–12 education is not a Progressive notion. If the Wisconsin Progressives of a century ago were here to observe the teachers union and the government bureaucracy fighting to preserve the current monopoly, I am certain it would remind them of the nineteenth-century trusts, and the powerful men who fought to preserve them. And so, ironically, the public school system cherished by Wisconsin Progressives has become like the monopolies they fought to dismantle. It is insulated from competition, highly resistant to change, and can treat its customers any way it wants. Like the monopolies of a century ago, it primarily serves its own interests rather than the people's interests.

Milwaukee Public Schools (MPS) is a good example. It is Wisconsin's largest and most urban school district, responsible for more than 10 percent of the state's public school students. In 1986, more than one-half of incoming high school freshmen were not graduating. Among African American males, the dropout rate was 80 percent. The mean grade-point average was a D-plus. A 1985 study commissioned by my predecessor, Governor Anthony Earl, found an "unacceptable disparity in educational opportunity and achievement" between poor and nonpoor children, and between white and nonwhite children. In a 1987 survey, 57 percent of public school teachers in the district said they wouldn't want their own children to attend the school where they taught.

Facing such a dismal failure of the public school system, a number of Milwaukee's African American political leaders began calling for a shakeup of the public school system. In 1987, Annette "Polly" Williams, a state representative whose district included the central city of Milwaukee, introduced an amendment to end forced busing in Milwaukee. For ten years, Milwaukee had been under court order to desegregate its schools. Busing African American children out of their neighborhoods to predominantly white public schools was the remedy the school district was applying to achieve desegregation. Approximately 90 percent of the children being bused were black.

Williams's amendment provided that busing could occur only if a child's parent or guardian specifically requested it in writing. "Don't they have a right to say they don't want their children on that bus?" she asked. Polly argued that the burden of desegregation was disproportionately falling on African American families and their children. She also blasted conventional notions about school desegregation. "I definitely do not feel integration is necessary for a quality education," she said. "There is an implication that in order for black children to learn, they have to sit next to white students. I refuse to accept that."

Polly's outspoken views stirred things up in Milwaukee and among the liberal, predominantly white, Wisconsin legislature. Polly had credibility. She was an African American Democrat—the chair of Reverend Jesse Jackson's 1988 presidential campaign in Wisconsin—who had grown up poor in the central city and had even been on welfare. She knew what she was talking about. Her proposal received strong support in Milwaukee's black community. The *Milwaukee Times*, a black-owned weekly, editorialized its support, saying, "Black students were the victims of unequal segregated schools and should not be the victims of the remedy."

The state assembly nearly passed her amendment, falling short by three votes. Rural Republicans had voted with her but the Democrat leadership did not, causing Polly to tell the press that "white liberals" had blocked her reform. Speaker of the assembly Tom Loftus—who three years later would run against me for governor—promised he would bring up the issue again in the next budget. And in true liberal fashion, he warned MPS that if improvements were not made, the state would "take over the schools."

In August 1987, Polly and an impressive group of community leaders announced a new proposal. It called for establishing a separate school district in Milwaukee's central city. This new, predominantly black school district would achieve Polly's goal of allowing children to attend neighborhood schools rather than being bused across town. The group lashed out at busing, arguing that "body shuffling" had done nothing to improve academic achievement among black students. "If the last thirty-four years of desegregation have proved anything, it is that busing to achieve 'racial balance' does not improve learning," they said.

In December I met with some of the group's members to discuss their idea. I was putting together my 1988/89 budget, and they wanted me to include their proposal. Polly was there, as well as Dr. Howard Fuller, who was dean of Milwaukee Area Technical College, and George Mitchell, an education consultant in Milwaukee who had been an appointee of a previous Democrat governor, Patrick Lucey. I had served with Polly in the state assembly and I liked her. But she was stubborn and independent like me. We were not philosophical soul mates.

I told the group that I didn't think the proposal to create a separate school district would work. Public schools come with a plethora of rules and regulations and bureaucracy. To me, the problem wasn't just busing, it was the public schools themselves. For years I had watched as the state and local property taxpayers had pumped millions of more dollars into the Milwaukee Public School system. It didn't get any better—it only got worse. The proposal to create a new school district was going to be expensive—there wasn't much of a property tax base in the low-income neighborhoods, so the state was going to have to kick in more money there, while continuing to send more tax dollars to the other Milwaukee public schools. In my view, it wasn't going to change the system. I wanted to try something new.

I said I wasn't inclined to support the proposal, but I did support the idea of neighborhood-based schools. Howard Fuller noted there were good schools in many of these low-income neighborhoods, but they were private schools, and most of them had a religious affiliation. I said, "Well, if those schools

are doing such a good job, and they're located in the neighborhoods where many of the children live, why not let the children attend those schools?"

That was a bombshell. It was clear that none of us had
really thought about this as a viable alternative. The first reaction was, "We can't do that, what about the public schools?" I
said, "What about the public schools? They aren't serving the
public. If a school can do a good job educating children, what
difference does it make who runs it?" "But what about the
cost?" someone asked. I pulled out the data. At that time, state
and local taxpayers were spending $5,222 to send each child to
public school. The cost at a private school was about half that
amount. "But if they're not going to public school, who will
decide where the kid goes?" they asked. "The parents," I said. I
didn't even have to think about it.

As we discussed the idea, it started to become clear that
school choice would accomplish what both they and I were trying to achieve. It would give parents more control and allow
children to attend the best schools in their own neighborhoods;
it would not cost the state any additional money, and it would
shake up the system. It was a simple, commonsense solution:
inject competition into the school system and let the market
work by empowering parents as consumers.

As the meeting ended, it was clear that Polly Williams was
not with me. She had put a lot of effort into her separate school
district proposal and was going to keep pushing it. I could tell I
had gained one key ally, though. Howard Fuller was intrigued
by the idea.

I did not have an ideological agenda in mind when I
decided to push for school choice. I was not being pressured by
conservatives or anyone else to do it. I basically stumbled onto
it by using my common sense. The private schools were doing a
better job, so why not try it on a limited basis? The people who
can afford to buy a house in a neighborhood where the best
public schools are located are usually the ones who can afford

to send their kids to private schools. Why should people with means have choice when poor people don't? I included religious schools in my proposal, not because I had a religious agenda, but because they constituted the bulk of private schools in low-income neighborhoods. I knew it was radical, but we had to be willing to try something very different because everything else had failed. The education lobby kept saying, "Reduce class sizes and give Milwaukee schools more money." But we had tried that. My predecessor and other governors had done that—class size had been reduced and Milwaukee had received more and more money. It didn't work.

Real change cannot happen in government unless you're willing to be bold. You might fail, but you've got to be willing to try something new. Nobody had tried this kind of solution. No one really knew how it would work or even if it would work. We were like scientists drawing equations on the chalkboard. But it made sense given the circumstances we were facing.

I also believed school choice in Milwaukee was not only related to, but an important building block of, our experiments with welfare reform. Learnfare required students on welfare to stay in school, but requiring children to attend bad schools wasn't going to help them accomplish anything in life. Milwaukee had the largest number of welfare recipients in the state. I didn't think my reforms would work without changing the public school system. Unless low-income families had good, solid educational opportunities, the welfare rolls could only go up.

When I told my staff I had promised to put private-school choice in my budget, I got a mixed reaction. My younger aides were excited and supportive. Some of my more senior aides didn't want me to do it. Some argued it would be a sure loser in the legislature. "Why set yourself up for defeat?" they said. Others felt it would brand me as a right-wing conservative in a state that had not been hospitable to such politicians. Ronald Reagan, they said, lost on his school voucher proposal and was hurt politically. But I had seen that too, and I respected him for trying. Although I knew it would be tough sailing in the Democrat-controlled legislature, I wasn't convinced I would lose. Polly Williams had started something with her anti-busing amendment earlier in the year. There was a coalition developing—there was support for fundamental reform among real people who were fed up with how the public school monopoly was treating them and their children.

In January 1988, I introduced school choice as part of my budget. The proposal allowed low-income Milwaukee children to attend any school of their choice, private or parochial. Low-income families could use for private school tuition a portion of the tax dollars that otherwise was being spent on their public school attendance.

When we put the proposal together, we didn't have any model from anywhere else to base it on, so we kept it very simple. We proposed that the state would write a joint check to the parents and the private school they chose. The state would pay the tuition charged by the private school, not to exceed $2,400, which was the per-student level of state aid that was currently being provided to MPS. (This was approximately one-half of the total per-student cost of the public schools. It did not include local property taxes that were also being used to fund the schools.)

My proposal was met with a resounding thud. The atheist Freedom From Religion Foundation, which is very active in Madison, assaulted the parochial school provision. Bert Grover, who headed DPI, immediately pronounced it dead, and the state teachers union called it an assault on public education. The Democrats who controlled both houses of the state legislature characterized it as the same old right-wing conservative agenda Ronald Reagan had pushed earlier. But what really torpedoed it was the lack of any significant grassroots support in Milwaukee's African American community. Without Polly Williams or other prominent community leaders on board, there was no movement from the people to make the change.

The Democrats easily killed school choice in the legislature's powerful Joint Finance Committee. It never even made it to the floor of the legislature for a vote.

That defeat was an important lesson for me. I realized I couldn't get choice passed on my own. It didn't matter how hard I worked or how sincerely I believed it was the right thing to do. A conservative, Republican, white male governor from Elroy wasn't going to change the Milwaukee school system without the support of the city's black leaders. If choice was going to be a reality, I needed to build a coalition that would include leaders from across the spectrum. And to do that I had to show that the idea could work.

I instructed my education adviser, Tom Fonfara, to begin working on a proposal for my next budget. Tom was bright, young—as most of my staff has been—and a strong believer. Since we definitely couldn't turn to DPI for help, Tom put together a working group on education that began fashioning a new choice proposal and other education reforms for my next budget. He also began the hard work of putting together a coalition of choice supporters from Milwaukee and around the state. I gave him a free hand to develop proposals and bring others on board. Periodically, he reported his progress, and we would discuss next steps, but he was in charge of leading the effort in my office.

In January 1988, I was invited to a White House Workshop on Choice in Education. It was one of the last events Ronald Reagan was to host at the White House, and President-Elect George Bush was attending. A broad range of national experts on choice was going to be there: Jeanne Allen from the conservative Heritage Foundation, John Chubb from the liberal Brookings Institute, and community-based empowerment advocates such as Robert Woodson, from the Center for Neighborhood Enterprise, and Joyce Duncan, who ran a public-school choice program in East Harlem, New York.

I was allowed to invite one guest, so I invited Polly

Williams. I gained a lot from the workshop, but I think Polly gained more. For the first time, I think she realized that school choice was not just a conservative Republican idea. There was a network of African American leaders at the grassroots level who were fighting for it—people like Bob Woodson, who had cut his political teeth in the civil rights movement. Both of us found a level of energy at that conference that we hadn't experienced before. It gave us optimism. School choice was doable if we could put the right coalition together. I told Polly that I was again planning to include school choice in the budget, and I asked for her support. She agreed. She wanted to lead the effort in the legislature.

In January 1989, I reintroduced school choice as part of my budget. We had taken parochial schools out of the proposal, although I still believed the program would be more successful with them. I knew from my previous experience that including religious schools brought out too many long knives, and I wanted to win this time. So I proposed allowing low-income families in Milwaukee to send their children to "nonsectarian" private schools. I also proposed separate legislation establishing public-school choice statewide. I did so because I believed competition would be good for the public schools. If parents wanted to send their children to a public school outside their district, I didn't see any reason that they shouldn't be allowed to do so. Rudy Perpich, the Democrat governor of Minnesota, had already implemented a successful public-school choice program in his state. I had spoken to him about it at the White House conference, and, of course, reminded him that anything Minnesota could do, Wisconsin could do better.

I thought my public-school choice proposal would be relatively noncontroversial. I was wrong. Nearly every education interest group in the state came out against it: DPI, the state teachers union, the state School Board Association, and the School District Administrators Association. DPI had concerns about all the administrative work it would have to do to sort out the funding when students moved from one district to another. The teachers union feared teachers might be laid off if students abandoned a particularly bad public school. Critics blasted Minnesota's experience, noting that only 5 percent of the students there switched schools. To them, that meant the program was a failure. To me, it meant the opposite. If 100 percent of the students in Minnesota had a choice and only 5 percent switched schools, their public schools must be doing a pretty good job—and wasn't it a good thing that parents and children were free to make that choice?

None of this opposition from the education establishment was unexpected. The real blow came from individual school board members and parents who didn't want it to happen. Wisconsin communities take a great deal of pride in their schools. People in small towns like Elroy tend to view their own schools more positively than the education system as a whole— "Public schools are going downhill, but our school is doing a good job." Many rural school districts didn't want "outsiders" coming into their schools, and they didn't see how choice was relevant to them. It may be something a big city like Milwaukee could use, but why is it relevant in Whitehall or Rice Lake? The clincher, though, was athletics. Parents and local school board members worried about recruiting wars in which other school districts would lure away their best athletes. When it comes to hurting the high school football team, you're asking for big trouble. So my public-school choice proposal died when school board members and superintendents—and football coaches and cheerleaders—from across the state called their legislators and said, "Don't do this."

Meanwhile, my private-school choice proposal was being beaten up by the usual suspects—not by parents but by DPI and the state teachers union. It became the lightning rod of my budget. The Democrat leaders in the legislature and the interest groups lambasted it. They called it an assault on public schools and gravely predicted it would siphon off the bright students to private schools while leaving behind the poor achievers in underfunded public schools. Both of Milwaukee's daily newspapers, the more conservative *Sentinel* and the liberal *Journal*, editorialized against it. According to them, I was turning my back on the public schools.

However, the largest black-owned newspaper in the state, the *Milwaukee Community Journal*, came out in support of it. Mikel Holt, the editor, wrote a powerful endorsement. This changed the equation. It was a glimmer of hope. Unlike a year ago, we had the support of an influential institution within the African American community. Nearly every week after the first editorial, Mikel Holt included something in the paper supportive of school choice. I would like to take credit for that and describe how that endorsement was the result of a careful strategy implemented by me and my staff. But it wasn't. We hadn't expected it.

Nevertheless, the legislature's Joint Finance Committee again removed the private-school choice proposal from my budget. The Joint Finance Committee routinely removed proposals from my budget it didn't agree with on the grounds that the proposals were policy matters that should be dealt with separately. Where the line is between policy matters and budget matters is highly subjective. Once items were removed from the budget, I could try to have them added back on the floor of the assembly or senate as an amendment to the budget bill, or passed as separate legislation, but this was difficult to accomplish with the Democrats controlling both houses.

With Joint Finance in charge of final committee approval of the budget, we had to reroute the proposal around the committee by introducing it as separate legislation. Polly was preparing to do that in the assembly. Fonfara began working with Larry Harwell of Polly's staff to help draft the legislation and line up votes. They also started talking with Walter Farrell, a highly respected professor at UW–Milwaukee who was working in the office of Senator Gary George, the chairman of the Joint

Finance Committee. Professor Farrell was receptive to the idea. While this was going on, MPS announced it too supported school choice, and offered its own plan. When Fonfara met with MPS representatives, however, it was clear they were playing politics. Under their plan, MPS would decide where kids would be assigned, not parents.

Polly introduced her bill in the assembly in October 1989 and it was referred to committee, with hearings set for February 1990. During this period, Polly and I and our staffs kept working to drum up support. She was meeting with community groups and speaking in Milwaukee's black churches, and I talked about the program in press conferences and speeches around the state. Tom Fonfara continued to work with Larry Harwell of Polly's staff to coordinate legislative and community support.

In early 1990, I introduced a series of funding bills for state agencies. The legislature had a limited period to act on these and any other pending legislation. It was scheduled to adjourn on March 28 and not return until January of the next year, after the November elections. Polly's school choice bill was scheduled for a vote in the assembly on March 13. Betty Jo Nelsen, the minority leader, was in charge of lining up all forty-two Republican votes, and Polly was responsible for bringing along enough of the fifty-five Democrats. Polly also invited to the assembly chambers a large group of low-income parents and children who wanted the freedom to choose their own schools. As the bill was being debated on the floor, the gallery was filled with these parents and children, watching and listening as members were about to vote. The measure passed 62–35. The people in the gallery made it easier for legislators to vote yes, and many Democrats considered it a "free vote." They were confident the bill would dead-end in the senate, which the Democrats controlled 20–13.

The glimmer of hope we had after passage in the assembly was quickly dashed by Senator Bob Jauch, who chaired the

senate education finance committee. He announced that the
bill would not even receive a hearing before the legislature
adjourned on March 28. We thought choice was dead. Our only
other option was going back to the Joint Finance Committee.
The committee had to approve the budget bills I had sent to it
in January. After the committee approved my budget measures,
both houses would vote on them as one large bill. Before sending the bill to the floor, however, the committee often added
amendments it deemed appropriate to pass. It took a vote in
both houses to remove such items from the budget once Joint
Finance put them in.

The committee was run by Senator Gary George, one of the
top leaders among the Democrats who ran the legislature. He
was also the only African American in the state senate, and his
district included many of Polly Williams's constituents. He had
blocked school choice twice before by removing it from my budgets, but things had changed since then. Polly had put together
a strong grassroots coalition of parents and community leaders
and had passed school choice in the assembly with the votes of
African American Democrat legislators from Milwaukee. And
the *Community Journal* had written a scathing editorial criticizing the senator after he removed choice from the last budget.
Senator George was getting some heat from his colleagues and
the voters back home.

On March 19, Tom Fonfara burst into my office and
reported, "Choice is in the budget." He had received a call from
Walter Farrell of Senator George's staff. The senator had
decided to add school choice as an amendment to the 214-page
budget bill the committee was going to pass. On March 21, the
committee passed its omnibus bill with school choice included.
On the same day, it was sent to the senate and assembly for
approval. Although amendments were offered in each house to
remove it from the budget, both failed. In the assembly, the
majority for choice already had been established on the March
13 vote. In the senate, Democrats did not want to take on

Senator George. After two years of effort, it was over that quickly.

Although the program was far-reaching, there were strict limitations on its size and scope. Participation was limited to children in low-income families who had not been enrolled in a private school during the previous school year. An overall limit on the number of participants was set at no more than 1 percent of the total school district student population. Enrollment caps were placed on individual schools, requiring that choice students could not exceed 49 percent of the school's total enrollment. The program was to end after five years, and only nonreligious private schools could participate. Moreover, private schools would not receive the full $6,222 per student in state and local tax dollars that the public schools now were spending. They would receive less than one-half that amount for tuition. Choice schools would receive tuition payments limited to the amount of per-pupil state aid going to the Milwaukee School District, which in 1990 was $2,446.

I vetoed the five-year limit on the program and signed the legislation into law on April 27. My approval of the choice experiment immediately kicked off a political firestorm. The Milwaukee chapter of the National Association for the Advancement of Colored People (NAACP), with the support of the state teachers union, filed suit in state court to block the reform. The state teachers union, white liberals, and the NAACP were fighting to keep low-income, predominantly African American families from picking their own schools. On the other side was an inner-city Democrat legislator aligned with a conservative Republican governor, joined by thousands of low-income parents fighting to give their children a better opportunity. It was an extraordinary departure from politics-as-usual.

The court challenge argued that the program violated the state constitution in three ways. First, the manner in which the legislation was passed violated procedural requirements for passing legislation as set forth in the constitution. (The legislation was passed as an amendment to the state budget bill, and the state constitution prohibits enacting "private or local" provisions as part of a "multi-subject" bill.) Second, the choice program failed to include sufficient state regulation. (Since private schools were not subject to the same regulations as public schools, opponents argued that "public" money was improperly being spent for "private" purposes.) And third, choice violated the constitutional guarantee of a "uniform" public education in Wisconsin. This third argument prompted Clint Bolick, a lawyer who represented low-income families seeking choice, to exclaim, "Does satisfying this constitutional provision mean everyone has to have a uniformly bad education?"

The irony of the NAACP leading the charge against school choice was not lost on Milwaukee's black community. The *Milwaukee Community Journal* asked NAACP head Felmers Chaney why the organization was the lead plaintiff in the lawsuit. Mr. Chaney replied that he hadn't actually read the plan. This response characterized much of the knee-jerk opposition to choice by liberals determined to preserve the status quo, even in the face of compelling commonsense reasons for trying something new. I've experienced this almost blind opposition to change in many of the reforms I've attempted in Wisconsin. Liberals who pride themselves on being open-minded and forward-looking have often fought tremendously to preserve the existing framework of government programs.

In addition to the court challenge, opponents tried to cripple the program by imposing new regulations on private schools participating in the program. This effort was led by Bert Grover at DPI. He extended state and federal regulations to the private schools set to participate in the choice program, without providing the funding that normally accompanies them. To comply with the new regulations, the private schools that had signed up for the program were facing bankruptcy, and they backed away from participating. Mr. Grover's actions got the attention of the

Wall Street Journal, which dubbed him the Orval Faubus of the 1990s for blocking the schoolhouse door to choice children.

In August, one month before the choice program was to begin running in Milwaukee, a Dane County circuit court upheld the constitutionality of the program on all counts. In addition, the court ruled that the private schools could not be regulated in the manner proposed by the state superintendent of public instruction. Although the legal arguments of choice proponents were strong, the court no doubt was also influenced by the busloads of low-income families from Milwaukee who jammed the courtroom to follow the proceedings. It was a compelling sight.

Choice opponents immediately appealed the circuit court ruling, and in November 1990, after children already had begun classes at choice schools, the court of appeals reversed the decision, ruling the program unconstitutional because it had been passed as part of a "multi-subject" budget bill. The program continued to run, however, as proponents appealed to the state supreme court. As during the earlier proceeding before the circuit court, Polly Williams arranged for buses from Milwaukee to transport low-income families to the supreme court in Madison to attend oral arguments. Unfortunately, the buses were late, and when the parents and children finally arrived, there was no room inside the chamber. Instead, the seats were taken mostly by union officials and workers from DPI who opposed choice, and various insiders both for and against the program. It was a poignant scene as the children pressed their faces to the glass windows of the doors to the state's highest court, on the outside looking in at a proceeding that would determine whether they would have the power to choose their own schools.

Finally, in March 1992, two years after the program had begun, the supreme court overruled the appeals court. In a 4–3 decision, the court found Wisconsin's first-in-the-nation private-school choice program constitutional.

In its majority opinion, the court captured the heart of the debate, ruling that school choice "empowers selective, low income parents to choose the educational opportunities that they deem best for their children. Concerned parents have the greatest incentive to see that their children receive the best education possible." And in a concurring opinion, Justice Louis Ceci wrote, "Let's give choice a chance. Literally thousands of school children in the Milwaukee school system have been doomed because of those in government who insist upon maintaining the status quo."

While the case had been working its way through the courts, the choice program was operating in Milwaukee. Although some schools and many families were scared off by the uncertainties created by the lawsuits, the program began in September 1990 with 341 low-income children attending seven private schools. By 1995, participation had increased by more than 200 percent, with 1,066 students enrolled in fifteen schools.

One of those schools is Bruce Guadalupe, a private school run by the United Community Center for first through eighth graders. Over the past few years, I have visited Bruce Guadalupe four times. In June 1991, I attended its commencement ceremony for twenty-five students graduating from the eighth grade. When I addressed the entire student body at the ceremony, I told the kids to come visit me at my office in Madison. The students and administrators just smiled politely and nodded their heads. A few months later, I hadn't heard from them. So I picked up the phone and called Walter Sava, the executive director of the United Community Center, and asked, "Where are the kids? Aren't they coming to visit?" Walter seemed surprised by my call. But sure enough, the kids were there in my office a few weeks later—and most of them got to spin around in my office chair a few times. The twenty-five students who graduated from Bruce Guadalupe in the ceremony I attended were already in high school at the time, so they didn't make it to my office with the rest of the kids. But we didn't lose track of them. In fact, just last year, each and every one of those Bruce Guadalupe graduates earned high school diplomas.

Studies evaluating the program have been conducted each year by University of Wisconsin professor John Witte, who was hired by DPI. The studies laid to rest the main argument choice opponents had used—that the program would skim the best students from the failing public schools. The opposite has occurred. Students participating in the choice program over-whelmingly are those who had been the lowest achievers in public school. And they are far more likely to be from single-parent families and on welfare. Although Witte has concluded, "It is not possible to reach a firm conclusion on achievement differences," he also has reported that "there is no systematic evidence that choice students do either better or worse than [public school] students." This has prompted choice opponents to rush to declare the program a failure. Yet, in a separate study, the nonpartisan Legislative Fiscal Bureau found that such a conclusion "is stronger than can be supported by the limited data available. In fact, no conclusion can be drawn." And another study by Harvard University professor Paul Peterson argues that choice students are doing better than before.

My view of the back-and-forth on achievement levels is this. Even if one were to accept Professor Witte's conclusion that there has been no measurable increase in academic achievement, choice has still been a solid success. If choice students are performing as well as public school students, they are doing so at one-half the cost of public schools. That in itself is no small accomplishment.

But school choice in Milwaukee has been a success for another, even more important reason. Those who have studied the program do not dispute the effect it has had on families: According to the studies, parents are very satisfied with their children's new schools, are more involved in the private schools than in their previous public schools, are more involved in their children's education at home, and have higher educational expectations of their children than parents whose children attend the public schools.

This, to me, is what makes the first phase of our choice experiment such an important success, and what holds the promise of education reform across America: the fact that it has empowered parents to play a more active role in the education of their children. Our limited experiment has given power back to ordinary people. The studies have found that choice is accomplishing its goal of reaching the most troubled, low-income students who had been lost in the public education system.

Despite the political upheaval generated by the choice program, it was a very modest experiment. By 1995, only 7 percent of low-income students in Milwaukee's poorest neighborhoods attended private schools. To pass the plan in 1990, we had to make compromises: a limit was placed on the percentage of choice students who could enroll at a private school. The limit was 49 percent (later increased to 65 percent). The effect of this cap was to create waiting lists at the most popular choice schools. Most choice students in Milwaukee were attending the three best nonsectarian private schools, and those schools couldn't accept more students. At the same time, though, good Catholic schools in low-income neighborhoods were under-utilized or shutting down. The low-income families who live in those neighborhoods, if they couldn't get their children into a private-school choice program, couldn't afford to send their children to the parochial schools. Instead, the children still were being bused to public schools.

We learned important lessons watching the program in operation and going through its growing pains. Enrollment caps were a problem. Consistently there was more demand than space. When one choice school shut down because it couldn't attract enough students, critics immediately said this showed the program was a failure. Funny, to me it showed the strength of the program. A school shut down because it couldn't attract customers. Government-run schools don't shut down due to poor performance—they get more money.

We had hoped the program would encourage new private schools to be created in low-income neighborhoods. This didn't happen. Enrollment limits played a role in this, as did the contentious political and legal battle over the program. I had vetoed the five-year limit on the program, but it wasn't clear if it would continue if I wasn't reelected. There were too many risks to starting a new school. And the funding level the state was providing—one-half the per pupil public school cost—was not sufficient to overcome the other risks.

Meanwhile, Milwaukee's public schools were continuing to fail—and the state and local property taxpayers were dutifully pumping in more money. The limited choice program was like a mosquito bite to the mammoth public school monopoly. There still was no real competition. Dr. Howard Fuller, who had met with me in my office in 1988 with Polly Williams and George Mitchell when choice was first discussed, was now superintendent of MPS. Even his efforts at reform were constantly being batted down by the education establishment. He asked for the authority to shut down failing schools, but the education establishment wouldn't let him. He proposed a standardized math test to determine what students were learning, but the teachers union wouldn't allow it. Dr. Fuller kept trying, and when he finally convinced the school board to allow the test, three-quarters of the students failed it. Although Dr. Fuller supported school choice, the Milwaukee school board prohibited him from speaking publicly in favor of it. That was the kind of system we were up against.

By 1994, it was clear to me that the limited school choice program had failed to create the competition necessary to improve public schools. Nor had it fully addressed the neighborhood school issue that had first prompted Polly Williams and others into action. Milwaukee still had a system of "separate and unequal" education in which the vast majority of low-income students were relegated to substandard public schools.

I knew we hadn't yet solved the problem. What had motivated me to act—and fight—for choice the first time still was
knocking at the door. Like my father in the grocery store, I
couldn't walk away from the problem—I needed to keep working on the solution. The challenge was to figure out a way to
accommodate all the low-income students who wanted to
switch to private schools. Nearly all of Milwaukee's 130 private
schools are religiously affiliated, and many of them are located
in low-income neighborhoods. By all objective measures, the
neighborhood-based religious schools were providing far superior education than public schools at less than one-half the
cost, yet many low-income children from those neighborhoods
still were being bused to inferior public schools miles away. Our
choice program needed to be expanded to include those
schools.

During my reelection campaign in 1994, I met with a group
of Milwaukee business executives and leaders of the city's
African American community. They told me that expanding
school choice was their number one priority for the next budget. When we had passed school choice in 1990, the business
community stayed out of the fight. Now, it was their top priority. The poor public schools—and the ill-prepared students they
sent into the workplace—were having a negative impact on
hiring. Business people saw school choice as a way to improve
their future. They argued strongly that religious schools had to
be included—without them there was no capacity to expand. I
promised I would propose an expansion of choice in my 1995
budget. A week before the election, I repeated that pledge at a
jam-packed rally for choice students in Milwaukee.

The Freedom From Religion Foundation notwithstanding,
it just made sense to match up the kids with the good schools in
their neighborhoods that needed students. To my mind, government was still too much in the way—limiting the number of
students who could participate, telling parents which schools

they could send their children to. The reins were too tight. If you followed the choice idea to its most logical conclusion, there was only one really good answer: drop caps; give parents a check; let them, not the government, decide.

When I announced the expansion of school choice to religious schools in February 1995, this is what I said to the legislature and the citizens of Wisconsin:

> School choice is more than a program. It is a philosophy. It is the belief that parents know best when it comes to their own children. It is the belief that poor parents have the same right to choose that other parents have. If a mother in Milwaukee wants her child to walk to the private school across the street instead of being bused to a public school across town she's going to have that choice. If that private school across the street has a religious affiliation she is still going to have that choice. Religious values are not the problem. Drop-out rates and low test scores are. Government currently is allowed to pay for whatever preschool a parent chooses. It is allowed to pitch in for whatever college they choose. It is only for kindergarten through high school that we assume bureaucrats know best. Not anymore.

One thing I've learned in a decade as governor is, "Success has many parents, failure has but one." When the choice program was first proposed, not many people were willing to give it a shot. It took a lot of hard work, learning, and talking to get local leaders and low-income families behind the idea. This time, the state legislature overwhelmingly approved the expansion, and I signed it into law on July 26, 1995. More than 3,500 students and eighty schools signed up for the program for the school year that began two months later. Before the program began operating, I visited a Catholic school in Milwaukee that was going to participate. A large group of parents and children who had signed up under the new choice law were there. One mother and father approached me. They were Hmong and spoke no English. But they brought an interpreter along just to say, "Thank you."

Yet, as before, choice opponents filed suit to block the program. In August, the American Civil Liberties Union and the state teachers union filed suit. The Wisconsin Supreme Court approved an injunction preventing 3,500 children from attending choice schools until the court ruled on the merits of the case. An eleventh-hour lawsuit blocked the schoolhouse door to low-income families who had already enrolled their children in better schools. (Ironically, a survey conducted about the same time revealed that one-third of Milwaukee public school teachers were sending their own children to private schools.)

The ACLU suit alleged that school choice expansion was an unconstitutional violation of the separation of church and state. I disagreed. The program gives no government funds to religious schools. It gives vouchers to low-income families to use at any school they choose. This is an important distinction. It is similar to other government assistance programs, the most successful of which was the G.I. Bill, which gave vouchers to U.S. servicemen after World War II to use at the school of their choice.

As before, low-income parents lined up to plead their case. Among them were Juan and Pilar Gonzalez, lifelong residents of Milwaukee trying to provide a good education for their four children: fourteen-year-old Leigha, eight-year-old Andrés, six-year-old Bianca, and two-year-old Tomás. Andrés was being picked up by the school bus at 6:50 A.M., transported to a school miles away, and returned home at 4:30 P.M. The school choice expansion would allow him to attend a Catholic school two blocks from his home. Mrs. Gonzales told the court:

> We pay over $2,000 per year in taxes to support the public education system, $2,000 of hard-earned money that is not effectively educating our children. We can't afford an additional $2,000 to send our kids to private schools to get the job done right. If this program is done away with, I will

find a way to have my children attend private school even
if it means less food on the table. A quality education for
my children is that important. Parents need to fight to get
a quality system back. That might take a while. But I need
quality education for my kids today.

Parents shouldn't have to choose between food and a quality education for their children. Another parent, Dinah Cooley,
asked the court not to block the expansion of school choice so
she could send her ten-year-old son Jetannue and three-year-old
daughter Shakevia to better schools. After listing examples of
violence and drug-dealing at her son's public school, she
expressed very simply what all parents want for their children.
"I want my children to attend private school because I think
they will learn more there and will have a better chance of
graduating from high school and becoming successful, produc-
tive adults." And she added, "If the program is struck down, I
will be forced to send my children to dangerous schools that do
not meet their educational needs."

Perhaps the most insightful argument for the expansion of
school choice came from Dr. Howard Fuller, who resigned as
superintendent of MPS in July after candidates backed by the
teachers union took over the Milwaukee school board. In his
candid, inside account, Dr. Fuller told the court that the public
school system "remains fundamentally mired in the status quo."
All but naming the teachers union and its allies in government,
he continued, "Powerful forces conspire to protect careers, contracts, and current practices before tending to the interests of
our children. Because of these forces, what we have achieved
has been painfully and unnecessarily slow in coming. I firmly
believe, based upon my experience, that school choice can
change that." And Dr. Fuller clearly identified the line that dis-
tinguishes choice proponents from the education establishment
when he told the court, "Although I strongly support public
education, in the final analysis, it is not the bureaucracy that is

important, it is the students. The question must be asked, what is in the best interest of the students, not what is in the best interest of the bureaucracy."

On Tuesday, February 27, 1996, the Wisconsin Supreme Court heard oral arguments on the case. Nationally, choice advocates dubbed the day "super Tuesday" because it coincided with the introduction of legislation in Congress to establish voucher programs for students in one hundred cities. The Clinton Administration responded by aligning itself firmly with the education establishment. With alarmist hyperbole I've heard a hundred times in Wisconsin, education secretary Richard Riley warned that private- and parochial-school choice could mean the death of public education. Choice programs like Wisconsin's, he warned, are "a retreat from the democratic purposes of public education." That would not make much sense to the Gonzalez family, Dinah Cooley, and thousands of other low-income families in Milwaukee.

On March 29, the Wisconsin Supreme Court deadlocked 3–3 on whether the choice expansion to include religious schools is appropriate under the state constitution. The court's nonruling sent the case down to the circuit court, but the case will likely wind up back in the state supreme court. Regardless of the outcome in Wisconsin courts, the case is all but certain to reach the U.S. Supreme Court to resolve the issue of whether school choice can include religious schools.

In cities across America, low-income, predominantly minority children are trapped in failing schools. What we are trying in Wisconsin, in Milwaukee in particular, will ignite a fundamental and necessary national debate over the future of public education in America. Must public education continue to be a government-run monopoly? Wisconsin has laid the foundation of a new model of public education in America, one in which public schools are not defined as government-run schools, but as schools that serve the public, regardless of who runs them.

Dramatic departures from the status quo cannot happen

overnight, particularly when reforms such as school choice threaten powerful entrenched interests who like things the way they are. Wisconsin's school choice success, though, shows that powerful special interests are really no match for ordinary people who join together to fight for change. When parents organize behind an idea and make their position known, politicians are loath to stand in the way. Our experience demonstrates how fiercely the current education establishment will fight to preserve the status quo, but it also shows how commonsense change can occur when political leaders put aside partisan differences and work together with ordinary people to fight against the monopoly.

To energize ordinary people and make the kind of changes America needs, political leaders have to be willing to lead. They have to stick their necks out and keep trying despite setbacks. When I first proposed private-school choice in 1988, it was not a popular thing to do. It was confrontational, and it failed to pass. But I came back with it in my next budget. I didn't quit. My team and I learned from our mistakes, we brought in critical players, and we never gave up. But it was not without cost. The state teachers union did everything in its power not only to politically defeat but also to personally hurt me, Polly Williams, and others who supported choice. But we kept on fighting, and in the end school choice passed a Democrat-controlled legislature with bipartisan support and prevailed in the courts.

My willingness to fight for what I believed in and the fact that we won the battle had a broad impact on the political landscape regarding education reform in my state. It showed that real change was possible, and that made the education establishment more eager to work together with me on other reforms. The school choice battle helped to establish the groundwork for important bipartisan reforms like school to work.

SCHOOL TO WORK

In Elroy, Wisconsin, where I grew up, most of the high school graduates do not go on to receive a college degree. Many go directly to work after high school, some on the farm, some in factories or construction, hoping to find well-paying jobs, which are tough to get without a specific skill. This almost was the path I took. After graduating from high school in 1959, I set off for Kenosha, Wisconsin, with four classmates, looking for work at American Motors. Three of us got jobs, and I wasn't one of them. The company told me I didn't have the aptitude for assembly line work.

The kids from Elroy who go looking for work after high school are not the exception but the rule throughout America. Nationwide, 73 percent of high school graduates do not go on to earn a four-year college degree. Why, then, do our schools, their facilities, faculties, and curricula focus so much on the other 27 percent? Probably because most of us have an innate bias in favor of sending our children to college. We want our children to be doctors or dentists, lawyers or teachers. Those were my aspirations for my own three children. But don't we have enough Ph.D.'s in history and political science tending bar and driving cabs? Common sense says our schools should continue to prepare students for college but should also teach real, marketable skills to help students get well-paying jobs, whether they go to college or not.

Our nation's public schools, K–12, are set up for an economy of the 1950s, when 60 percent of the labor force was unskilled. By the year 2000, only 15 percent of America's labor market will be unskilled.

I started thinking seriously about changing the mission of Wisconsin public schools soon after I took office in 1987. My wife, Sue Ann, had numerous stories about young people who were graduating from high school without any marketable skills. Many students held jobs while they were in school, but there was no connection between what they were learning in school and what they were doing at work. As a teacher, she was frustrated with what she saw as gaps in the education system. During their junior and senior years, most students were just hanging around waiting to graduate. Sports and socializing were important to them, but the academic part of school was becoming irrelevant. Some were planning to go on to college, and others couldn't wait to get out and start making money. They put in their time, earned their diplomas, and went to work, most at minimum wage. They had no job-ready skills to command a high-paying job in Wisconsin's growing manufacturing industry. They gave little or no consideration to a career path while in high school, and had received no formal skills training either in the classroom or on the job. They had a high school diploma, but it said nothing to potential employers about any particular skills, training, or aptitudes that would make them a good hire.

I was hearing from business and labor leaders concerned about a shortage of skilled labor in the state. During my first two years as governor, I had made several important policy changes to help revive Wisconsin's moribund economy. We cut income taxes, cut capital gains taxes, and changed the anti-business attitude of state government. In almost every speech, I talked about jobs and the importance of making Wisconsin a pro-business state. As the economy started to respond, businesses expanding in the state and companies that had relocated to Wisconsin came to me and pointed out a serious problem: they needed more skilled workers. Labor leaders also were sounding the alarm. The workers being turned out by our schools didn't have the basic skills to command well-paying jobs. They were facing a skills gap too, which meant fewer union workers or lower wages for workers in the long run.

This bothered me. On one hand, we were working hard doing the right things to create more jobs and more opportunities for people. But on the other hand, government wasn't doing its job of helping people capitalize on those opportunities. Our schools were disconnected from the realities of our changing economy. They were spending a lot of money "educating" students, but they were not giving our children the tools they needed to succeed in the real world. There had to be a change.

In 1989, President Bush invited me to an education summit of all the nation's governors in Charlottesville, Virginia. I invited Bert Grover, our state school superintendent. We were in the middle of a very public battle over school choice at the time, but we were not enemies on a personal level. Bert was a Democrat and had been elected statewide to head DPI. We had similar upbringings and a take-no-prisoners approach to our jobs, but he was more closely aligned with the educational establishment. I was hoping this trip would help us build a relationship.

Bert had already been working to move Wisconsin schools toward a school-to-work model. He had studied the research showing an approaching skills gap in the nation's workforce. He had talked with businesses about what they needed that Wisconsin schools were not teaching. He had started an Education for Employment program to begin nudging school districts to create partnerships with businesses at the local level and begin developing work-based standards that could better prepare students for work. Although the president's education summit did not deal directly with school to work and youth apprenticeships, Bert and I talked about our ideas for setting up a program in Wisconsin.

A short time later, Grover invited my top aide, Jim Klauser, to Germany to learn about that country's extensive school-to-work program in operation. Klauser and Grover were given tours of schools, businesses, and labor organizations. They saw firsthand a dynamic youth apprenticeship program that was helping young people become successful workers. There was no "downtime" in the German education system. Some 70 percent of high school students were participating in one of several different apprenticeships. It was not just a government program, it was a societywide partnership involving business, labor, and schools. Everyone had a role. Business and labor jointly established industry standards and determined the skills youth apprentices needed to learn to perform high-skilled jobs. The schools provided curriculum and classroom teaching to match those skill requirements, and businesses provided on-the-job training to round out the curriculum. There was healthy communication and regular, often contentious, debate among the three institutional partners, but all had the same goal of preparing young people for successful careers.

German schools also had an important institution that didn't exist in our schools. Nearly every school was affiliated with a career counseling center, a hub of activity where young people learned about job and training opportunities. In Wisconsin schools, guidance counselors were spending only about 3 percent of their time on career counseling. In German schools, every student began a formal process of exploring career options after the sixth grade.

Klauser came back from Germany interested in examining ways to set up a similar program in Wisconsin. To begin that process, we needed to get more people involved: people from our state Department of Industry, Labor, and Human Relations; and business leaders like Jim Haney, who ran the Wisconsin Manufacturers and Commerce Association, and John Torinus Jr., who owned a growing printing business that needed more skilled labor. John Torinus offered to help set up a youth apprenticeship in his company. We wanted the people who would actually run such a program in Wisconsin to learn from a model that was working, so we secured funding from a private foundation for a more broadly based study trip and in the fall of 1990 sent a team of business leaders, labor leaders, and government officials back to Germany. They observed a specific apprenticeship in printing from start to finish to learn how the different players fit together to make the system work. They learned how a carefully constructed series of tasks and duties mastered over a period of several years earned the student a certificate of occupational proficiency.

In that same year, Dwight York, who headed our system of sixteen state technical colleges, helped me set up the Governor's Commission for a Quality Workforce. The efforts to establish a school-to-work system in Wisconsin had been fragmented. Almost a decade earlier, there had been some efforts to integrate the colleges with the public schools. A limited number of high school students had been taking courses at technical colleges and receiving credits toward their diplomas. A 1990 commission composed of private sector leaders had recommended expanding school-to-work efforts statewide. The governor's commission served as a practical tool to synthesize the various proposals and create a focal point for moving forward with a specific program we could implement because it was backed by the governor and a bipartisan membership. The commission was headed by Carl Weigell, a Wisconsin businessman who had made the second study trip to Germany with Klauser and Grover. Meanwhile, Bert Grover had been aggressively promoting related programs at DPI and working to build acceptance for the idea in the education community.

The commission included one Democrat and one Republican legislator, the president of the state AFL-CIO, several business leaders, and representatives from state government and the public schools. It pulled together all the data pointing out the need for a system of skills training for our schools: surveys from businesses on what they were looking for, facts on the growing demand for and expected shortage of skilled American workers, and information about what Wisconsin schools were doing and not doing to meet those demands. In April 1991, the commission issued its report, with specific ideas for promoting youth apprenticeships and enhancing and expanding technical-based curricula in the state's public schools. It also called for new links between the state's technical college system and K–12 public schools. The two legislators who served on the commission, Representative Rick Grobschmidt, a Democrat, and Senator Margaret Farrow, a Republican, introduced a bill to establish a statewide system of school to work and the first youth apprenticeship program in the nation.

Although the legislation was broadly supported, there were some wrinkles that had to be worked out before passage. State labor unions were wary of the youth apprenticeship program. Since the early 1900s, the state had operated an apprenticeship program for adults. It had been established in 1911 as part of our Progressive Era reforms, and it was the first of its kind in the nation. The adult apprenticeship program was run by our Department of Labor, and the unions relied on it to run their own apprentice programs.

Organized labor was concerned that the youth apprenticeships might displace some of their long-established programs. I asked Bert Grover to bring them on board. He had taken Jack Reihl, the president of the state AFL-CIO, on one of his early study trips to Germany, which had helped bring labor along this far. But he had to keep working with Jack to get labor's support for the youth apprenticeship program. Eventually, they hammered out a compromise in which the statutory language creating the youth apprenticeship program emphasized its different and distinct purpose from the adult apprenticeship program. Assurances were given that youth apprenticeships would not compete with adult union-based apprenticeships. After that, organized labor did not oppose the legislation and in fact has been a partner in making the program work in Wisconsin.

There was also some concern about the program locking students into a particular career path at an early age or "tracking" them so some would be funneled into technical training instead of college. I made it very clear that, unlike the German system, we would not create separate tracks. The program would supplement, not displace, traditional college preparation coursework. Students who planned to go on to college could participate in job-related skills training, and students who planned not to earn a four-year degree would still have to complete their academic work. In fact, we made it possible under the program for any high school junior and senior to take college courses for high school credit.

Management of the youth apprenticeship program would be handled by the state Labor Department, rather than DPI. To be successful, I believed the program had to be industry-driven. Wisconsin's Department of Industry, Labor, and Human Relations was better suited for that. Local schools had to play a role, but I didn't want the education bureaucracy turning the program into mush. The teachers union didn't like this at all, but I insisted on it. Although Bert Grover would have preferred giving DPI the authority, he didn't oppose me. He knew and respected our labor secretary Carol Skornicka, and he understood the importance of avoiding turf wars on this issue. From what he had learned in Germany, he realized that business and labor had to take the lead role.

After overwhelming approval of the program by both houses of the legislature, I signed school to work into law. Although Bert Grover had made sure the state teachers union did not oppose the program, the union was not enthusiastic about it. It was used to developing its own curricula—and setting its own rules. Sharing that responsibility with interests outside the education system—business and the trade unions—meant giving up some power. There have been only a few legislative changes to the program since 1991. Most significantly, in 1993 we authorized the creation of career counseling centers in communities around the state, based on what we learned from studying them in Germany.

In addition to expanded technical courses in public schools and more integration with technical colleges, the initiative is providing high school students with on-the-job training in a private industry. Students learn by doing. They work outside school in a real business to gain real-world skills. Business and labor participate by working with schools to set up youth apprentice programs in communities across the state.

Of all the things I have done in ten years as governor, I am proudest of our youth apprenticeship program. During their junior and senior years, high school students are given the opportunity to work in a trade to gain a job skill employers are looking for. They take regular classes in the morning, and in the afternoon they work as printers or machinists or lab technicians or in other jobs for private businesses. The students are paid no less than minimum wage and work with a "mentor" on the job site who helps train them as youth apprentices. A mother of a high school student who participated in the program told me, "Our son comes home and speaks about 'his company' and 'his job.' This program has made a big difference . . . it has increased his ability to make something of himself." Students who successfully complete their apprenticeship receive something more than a diploma when they graduate. They also receive a certificate of mastery in a particular trade. This is a piece of paper that says something everyone can understand: they are high school graduates with a marketable skill.

When we enacted the statute starting youth apprenticeships statewide, we were the first state to do so. We started out small in 1992 with twenty-one students working as printing apprentices for nine employers in two communities. John Torinus, who had been on one of those early study trips to Germany and later played a key role on the Governor's Commission for a Quality Workforce, helped hire and train some of the first apprentices in his printing business. One of them, Paul Nurkala of West Bend, had been getting B's and C's in his regular coursework, but that changed to A's and B's when he started his apprenticeship in printing. "The main advantage," he said, "is it leaves me a step ahead of the guys coming out of high school because I can run a one-color press."

A year later, the number of students in the program grew to 157, an increase of more than 600 percent. We added another industry skill area—financial services—and the number of participating businesses rose more than 700 percent to seventy-seven, in six different communities. By the 1995/96 school year,

forty-three communities across the state had started apprenticeships in 490 different businesses for 881 students in the following skill areas: printing, financial services, manufacturing
machining, health care, architecture drafting and design, auto
collision repair, biotechnology, hotel and motel operations,
automotive technology, engineering drafting and design, insurance, mechanical drafting and design, and manufacturing and
production technology.

In 1996, I met with Jack Smith, the chairman of General
Motors (GM) Corporation in Detroit. GM was planning to start
German-style apprenticeships in automotive technology involving 40,000 to 50,000 apprenticeships nationwide. Wisconsin was
the only state in the nation with a youth apprenticeship in automotive technology. The program had enrolled 107 students, a
drop in the bucket compared to what GM was aiming for, but
still the chairman was asking us to help him set up programs in
all fifty states based on the Wisconsin model. We're doing that
now, and also bringing in Ford and Chrysler. We had taken a
simple idea and made it work. And now it can create real opportunities for thousands more people. That is what government
can do when it has the flexibility and willingness to experiment
with new ideas.

To make school to work successful, we had to ensure a
strong local and community-based role. From a practical perspective, I don't think the program would be successful if the
state government dictated procedures to businesses and communities. From a political perspective, it would have been
unwise to try to usurp local control of schools. So, for example,
we provide grants—which include federal grants—to local partnerships so they can develop their own youth apprenticeships.
Demand is very high. In 1994, we received more than one hundred applications from local partnerships.

Wisconsin's school-to-work program works precisely because
it is a partnership among government, local schools, parents,
businesses, and organized labor. The real work of the initiative is

done by labor, business, parent, and school groups in local communities across the state. State government plays the role of catalyst rather than micromanager. In our entire state government, only twenty employees are assigned to the school-to-work program. This is the commonsense versus government-sense model. There is no heavy-handed command and control regulatory apparatus—the government urges change, facilitates it, but doesn't prescribe or order how that change must occur. We leave that up to the people who create the jobs, protect the workers, and raise and teach the children.

The program also works because it has bipartisan support. While DPI chief Bert Grover and I differed on school choice, we were able to work together to achieve something we both believed was good for children. That kind of cooperation is hard to find in Washington. In Wisconsin, it is part of our Progressive tradition. Even though we have differences, we share a commitment to an ideal that state government can and should work.

Wisconsin is one state that over the past decade has taken important steps toward redefining the relationship between citizens and their schools. With changes like private-school choice and school to work we are creating schools that actually serve the public.

Wisconsin's experience suggests it will take a combination of reforms to move America's public education system into the twenty-first century. In my experience, there has never been a silver bullet—no one single solution to improving education, or, for that matter, protecting the environment, creating jobs, or helping people get off welfare. I have used a mixed approach to education reform. My solutions have not always met the ideological litmus tests of either conservatives or liberals. Experiments with education reform demonstrate that power really can be shifted back to people. School choice has put parents back in charge of their children's education, and school to work has given communities a greater role in teaching children.

CHAPTER FIVE

BALANCING BUDGETS AND CUTTING TAXES

E very year, governors, state legislators, and everyday citizens watch as the president and Congress try to work out a budget. Time after time, promises to balance the budget go up in smoke as the legislation winds its way through the Washington political process. One party wants this; one special interest will accept no less than that. No one in Washington is ever held accountable for the bottom line. If they try to cut, they're accused of being cruel Republicans. If they raise taxes, they're accused of, well, raising taxes. It must be worse to be accused of being a Republican, because collecting more taxes has been Washington's only consistent strategy. In 1950, the average family paid only 5 percent of its income to the federal government. To fund a 3,000 percent increase in federal spending since then, Washington now extracts 25 percent of an average family's income. This same American family's largest monthly expenses—greater than food, shelter, and medical care combined—are now federal, state, and local taxes.

Despite its repeated tax increases, the federal government is swimming in debt. A child born in 1996 will pay nearly $200,000 in taxes during his or her lifetime just for *interest* on the national debt. Not for Social Security, health care, national defense, roads, or anything else—but for interest on the national debt alone.

States (forty-nine of them) are bound, by their own constitutions, to achieve balanced budgets. They have no choice. In some states, as in Washington, increasing taxes has been viewed as a tool for balancing budgets. During the past ten years, twenty-eight states have increased sales or income taxes. (Wisconsin is the only state in the nation that has cut taxes, not increased any general tax rates, and balanced its budget every year since 1987.)

During the two decades before I became governor, state government spending in Wisconsin increased by an average rate of 10 percent a year. Once ranked thirty-first among all states in total spending, Wisconsin had risen to thirteenth by 1984. Higher and higher taxes were taking a toll on businesses and individuals. We were taxing ourselves poor. People—our most valuable resource—were moving out of the state. In 1986, Governor Earl established a special task force, the Wisconsin Expenditure Commission, to examine the tax and spending patterns and come up with long-term recommendations. I think he hoped this would diffuse criticism, but in the end, the report accentuated it—providing the hard numbers that showed just how bad the problem was.

As a candidate in 1986, I told people I would control government spending and cut taxes. It may not have been the most original platform in my campaign—Ronald Reagan had won election and reelection with this theme—but it really was the bedrock of my thinking. It was the most commonsense thinking I knew. I put out an issue paper that said, "Government spending drives taxes. That is a simple truth most politicians have lost sight of recently. We face a fiscal crisis because of our excessive government spending." I told voters that "the goal of the Thompson Administration will be to bring state spending in line with our ability to pay." This was a fundamental departure from the fiscal policy the government had followed for years, in which the government first decided what it wanted to spend and then raised the necessary taxes to pay for the programs. I turned that on its head, promising to determine our revenue levels first and then limit spending to the revenues we actually had. There would be no more credit-card spending.

The state was facing a revenue shortfall of $175 million— the spending we had committed to far outstripped the revenue that was coming in. The experts in government and the media all agreed another tax increase was necessary to balance the budget. They proclaimed it would be irresponsible for me to honor my campaign promise to cut taxes.

No one had paid much attention to my issue papers at the time—people are cynical about the promises candidates make during an election. But I intended to do exactly what I had promised. When people realized that the campaign papers were going to be the blueprint for the budget, there was a great skirmish among the media and various agencies to get hold of them. (Apparently they had lost or discarded their original copies.)

Actually creating a budget—not just talking about one—is the hardest thing I have ever done. There are literally thousands of decisions that must be made. In 1986/87, President Ronald Reagan was halfway through his second term. He had cut taxes, which had helped to spur economic growth. Revenues to the federal treasury had risen dramatically. Still, the Congress had passed and Reagan had signed into law federal spending increases that far outpaced the growth in revenues. Even a guy from Elroy knows a deficit when he sees one. Democrats (who had pushed for the higher spending) and the national media (who seemed to delight in the outcome) were constantly pronouncing Reagan's supply-side approach a failure.

To my mind, the president had gotten it half-right.

I wasn't going to cave in on tax cuts. I believed they were necessary to revive Wisconsin's sluggish economy. Cutting taxes would help bring jobs and people back to the state—and more jobs for more people translates into more revenues. It looks like a short-term money loss, but it's a long-term grand slam.

And I wasn't going to cave in on spending cuts. In reality, the necessity of cutting spending was established by my rock-bottom commitment to cut taxes and not bow to legislative pressure to raise them. If you say no to tax increases and you have a balanced budget requirement, you *have to* cut spending. It changes the whole dynamic. We were only going to buy what we could afford. We were going to have to make choices. In retrospect, people have said that Reagan had to spend a lot of money on defense—something I didn't need to account for in my budgets. But I know a lot of people who run up credit card bills with purchases of things they want but don't exactly need—like new clothes, cameras, and all sorts of indulgences. Maybe it's just human nature. If you have a credit card, if you can buy now and pay later, you often will. If that's the case, the best thing to do is to cut up the credit cards.

This was the scenario my team and I were facing. Even though I had won my election, the Democrats still held both houses of the state legislature. And they had been preparing a budget for a year with my predecessor, his philosophy, and their credit cards.

We had six weeks.

We started simply with the revenues we had. I said, "Subtract $100 million for tax cuts," and we went from there.

There was an assortment of taxes to target. An income tax cut would help to attract people and businesses back to the state, and so would more incentives for people to invest their money in the state and create more capital. The federal government had just eliminated the 60 percent exclusion of capital gains income from federal taxes. The Democrats in the state legislature were prepared to incorporate that change into Wisconsin's tax code, as other states were planning to do. I saw it differently. Here was an opportunity to make Wisconsin more competitive. Retaining the 60 percent exclusion would give us a leg up on other states in attracting investments and entrepreneurs. So we included the capital gains tax exclusion and a reduction in income tax rates in the budget I was to submit to the legislature.

I was determined to undo onerous inheritance and gift taxes. Wisconsin's collection rate in these areas was 72 percent higher than the national average. So people who had lived and worked in Wisconsin made a commonsense decision: to retire somewhere else. They left so their children and grandchildren could avoid paying such exorbitant taxes. (Undoubtedly, some were leaving to escape Wisconsin's winters, but they weren't coming back to enjoy our spectacular summers!) We were losing revenue, but, more important, we were losing a lot of talent and wisdom.

I used to tell people when I was on the campaign trail, "Please don't die and please don't move. Just hold on until I can be elected governor." The line always drew a knowing chuckle.

The other tax I knew we had to tackle was the property tax. In Wisconsin, property taxes are used primarily to fund public schools. They are assessed, collected, and spent at the local level. Public school costs had increased so dramatically in the decade before I became governor that, by 1986, rising property taxes were literally driving people from their homes and preventing young families from buying a first house.

During the campaign, I promised to increase the state's share of local education funding to 50 percent, up from the existing level of 46 percent. The theory was, if the share of state aid to schools was increased, local property taxes would go down, because state aid would replace school spending funded by the property tax. To make that really work, however, we had to place controls on school spending. Otherwise, schools could spend the additional money in state aid and continue increasing their share of spending from property taxes as well. This had been the pattern over the previous decade. The state share of education funding had increased, but so did property taxes, as the schools kept spending at rates exceeding what they were receiving.

Here was a clear-cut connection between taxing and spending. We proposed spending controls on schools, as part of our effort to "buy down" property taxes. At the same time, we increased state aid to schools by $131 million, as the first step in a four-year plan to reach a level of 50 percent state funding. With this increase in state aid, property taxes would go down if schools held spending increases to the rate of inflation. If school spending increased beyond that amount, property taxes would continue to go up, regardless of the state's increased contribution.

The various agencies had all been preparing their usual requests and spending projections for many months before I was elected. The agencies submit these requests to the Department of Administration (DOA), where a team of budget analysts review them to prepare the governor's budget. When I appointed my cabinet members, I gave them new marching orders. There were a few places I knew we would have to increase spending—for example, school aid and state employee pay increases that were locked in under contracts signed before I became governor. Inflation had to be taken into account as well. My commitment to cutting taxes narrowed the possibility of growth in spending. We could increase overall spending by the rate of inflation, but no more.

I asked my newly appointed cabinet secretaries to submit a budget spending only 95 percent of what their agency had spent in the previous year. This "reduced base" budgeting approach forced each agency to think about its priorities, about what its central, do-or-die role was. When I instructed them to make two more lists—one for programs they would add back if they could spend the same amount as last year, and another if they could spend 3.5 percent more—I got a sense of what was truly at the top of their to-do lists, if they became more efficient.

I gave each agency a choice: if you don't make the cuts, I'll make them for you. They soon discovered it was better to do it themselves. Nearly four hundred state employee positions were eliminated in twenty-four agencies. School aid and state employee compensation were the only programs that received increases above inflation. All other programs were held to an average increase of less than one-half of 1 percent. Altogether, the budget proposed a 3.6 percent increase in state spending, which was the projected rate of inflation.*

My budget caused a stir when it arrived in the legislature. The Democrats were waiting for it. I had surprised everyone by winning the governor's race. Because I had received only 53 percent of the vote, most of the Democrats figured it was a fluke and I'd be a one-termer. The budget was their first chance to prove that they were still in charge, and they set upon it like predators.

But I had something in mind that they weren't fully anticipating: the governor's veto power. This was a pair of scissors I could use to cut up the legislature's credit card. Wisconsin's governor has one of the strongest veto powers of any chief executive in the nation. It's not just a line-item veto, but a "partial" veto. It allowed me to cross out individual words and even letters and digits in spending bills passed by the legislature. And unless the legislature overrides a veto by a two-thirds vote of each house, the governor's changes become law.

I was prepared for the Democrats eliminating my tax and spending cuts, but at the same time I was convinced I would win on those issues if I confronted them. When you campaign for office, you get a very good sense of what people are thinking. Talking and listening to people is an infinitely better measure of public sentiment than a public opinion poll; for me, anyway. I had listened to thousands of people during the campaign. They really were fed up with the high taxes and spending. That's one of the key reasons they elected me. So if the liberals wanted to increase spending and taxes, and alienate people even more, I

---

*In this and every subsequent budget, I gave each cabinet secretary the opportunity to appeal the spending decisions I had made, before I submitted the budget to the legislature. However, under the "reduced base" budget procedure we had established, any secretary asking for more spending had to find the savings somewhere else in the budget to pay for it. The budget had to balance, and everyone understood that tax increases were not an option.

was happy to veto their changes to my budget. I said I was going to need a very large pencil to eliminate all the spending and taxes the legislature was adding. I was hoping the Democrats would get the hint.

After the budget passed the legislature with their changes, it came back to my desk. I had twenty-nine days to review the 893-page document, veto what I didn't like, and then sign it into law. The legislature had added several million dollars in spending, pared back my capital gains tax cut, created a new "alternative minimum tax," and thrown in a new tax on corporations. I began a series of meetings to decide what to veto. Generally, my predecessor had accepted what the legislature changed in his budget—he usually forwarded a few dozen vetoes, most of them technical in nature. Previous governors had challenged the legislature on some major policy issues, but usually their vetoes were few.

When I asked DOA budget analysts to identify *every single change* the legislature had made to my budget, they began to understand that I was going to do things differently. It was a massive undertaking. Rick Chandler, who was now state budget director, instructed the budget analysts to prepare a briefing document summarizing each of the legislature's changes and recommending whether I should veto it. The analysts then came to my office and we went through them one by one, day in and day out, including weekends and evenings.

As we went through each of the items, I wanted to know more than whether I should accept or veto the particular provision. In many cases, it wasn't a simple yes-or-no situation. I wanted to figure out how I could use the partial veto to revise what the legislature had done. I'd tell a budget analyst, "I want to accomplish this result," and she would say, "I'm not sure that you can." We put aside the summary recommendations prepared by the DOA and looked at the specific language of that particular provision in the budget bill to see how I could cross out words or letters to accomplish what I wanted. It soon became clear to the analysts that their summaries were not enough—they had to have the specific language from the budget bill with them as well. Not only did they have to know their facts and figures, they had to be innovative.

Jim Klauser and Rick Chandler had been with me through the campaign. They knew what I had promised and what keeping those promises meant to me. So during the veto sessions, they would chime in during the discussion of a particular item and say, "Remember, this is what we said during the campaign."

I also invited the public into the governor's office to discuss what they thought I should veto. For example, there was a small provision in the budget that affected taxidermists. I invited a group of taxidermists in to tell me what they thought about it. People were honored to have the governor ask them to come in, and invariably many brought members of their families along to meet me. My office became Grand Central Station. Over a two-week period I had budget analysts meeting in my office, and at the same time, public groups meeting with my staff in two other conference rooms. I shuttled from room to room, talking with all of them. After I finished with one group, another one came in. I had scheduled fifteen-minute blocks to spend with each group, but it always took longer. The meeting process went on until nine or ten at night, because people wanted to give me advice on the whole budget, not just the provision that affected them. I encouraged this, even if my staff would roll their eyes as a taxidermist and his wife would start giving me their ideas on welfare reform at the end of a long day. Taxidermists pay taxes too.

It was an exhaustive but important process. A forum was being provided, and people were taking advantage of the opportunity. I listened and learned. It reminded all of us that our budget decisions weren't just about agencies and numbers. They had an impact on the lives of real people.

I exercised the veto to cut $33 million in spending that the legislature had added, and eliminated the tax increases they had passed. Although there were many vetoes, I was more surprised by what I didn't have to change. Despite some grousing and efforts to alter my proposed tax cuts, the legislature approved both an income tax cut and the phase-out of inheritance and gift taxes. We had more of a fight on the capital gains tax cut. I had proposed excluding 60 percent of capital gains from taxation. The legislature cut it back. Using my veto power, I restored the 60 percent exclusion of capital gains and eliminated the two new taxes the legislature had passed, before signing the budget into law.

I could not use the veto to restore the school spending controls I had proposed to reduce property taxes. The legislature had removed them entirely from the budget, so there was no language I could modify to add them back in. All I could do was approve the increase in state aid to local schools in an effort to move closer to the 50 percent level I had promised during the campaign.

I held a press conference to announce my vetoes. There were 290 in all—far more than any governor had done before. Anticipating these vetoes, Cloyd Porter, a Republican legislator from Burlington, had presented me with a giant pencil made from a five-foot long four-by-four, courtesy of the Burlington Lumber Yard. Before the press conference, he had a shorter version made to reflect how much I had used the first one. I brought them both to the press conference to show the media. It made an impression, as did this statement I sent to the legislature with my vetoes:

> I ran a campaign to change the direction of Wisconsin state government. The budget I gave to the legislature last February emphasized the themes I campaigned on: more jobs, reducing taxes, controlling spending, and helping people get off welfare. With my vetoes, I've kept my commitment to the voters.

Democrats in the legislature were shocked by the number of vetoes and began an effort in the senate to override them. They blasted me in the news for "abuse of power." Since no governor had used the veto so extensively, an attitude had grown up that it should be used sparingly. I knew I was pushing the envelope, but I never doubted I was doing the right thing. I was using the power of the executive provided by the constitution, and the legislature had the power to override my decisions. That's how the balance of power was calibrated. If we were truly going to change the direction of tax and spending policy in Wisconsin, I felt I needed to send a strong message to the legislature: there was a new captain on board, setting a different course.

Ironically, although legislators liked to rail publicly about abuse of power, many of the items in their budget were not arrived at "democratically." Powerful committee chairmen had inserted a number of items into the giant budget bill and required their party members to toe the line. This was clear on some of the senate's twenty-six attempts to override my vetoes. On the capital gains tax cut, for example, only fifteen senators voted to override my veto and eighteen voted to sustain it. Not only did it fall far short of the necessary two-thirds support (twenty-two votes), it even fell short of a simple majority—four Democrats voted with me, against the position of their own party leadership.

In the end, none of my 290 vetoes was overridden. Standing up to the legislature had worked, and I hoped it would think twice before sending me more taxes and spending. I signed into law a budget establishing the third lowest spending rate in twenty-five years and a $100 million cut in taxes. The state was heading in a new direction.

DRAWING THE LINE

Although I continued to spar with the legislature over taxes and spending during my next two budgets—particularly on the issue of property taxes and my continued insistence on capping local school spending to reduce them—the next decisive battle came four years later, in 1991, after I had been elected to a second term with 57 percent of the vote. The state economy was performing well, state spending was under control, and we had avoided any increases in state tax rates. In this four-year period, revenues to the state increased by $1.1 billion, and by 1991, we had a $139 million budget surplus.

The Democrats, still in control of both houses of the legislature, had had enough. They proposed and passed a series of tax and spending increases. It was as though the previous four years had not even happened—a testimony to government's enormous ingrained appetite for more spending. Government doesn't like being restrained. It wants to spend money—like someone who's been given a credit card and doesn't have to pay the bill.

Representative Wally Kunicki, who had just been elected speaker of the state assembly, launched the Democrats' new tax and spending initiative. He announced an alternative budget with $700 million in new taxes and proudly proclaimed, "It's a great day to be a Democrat." Kunicki made his announcement on a Saturday. I immediately assembled my top budget advisers—Jim Klauser, Rick Chandler, Christopher Mohrman, Scott Jensen, and Bill McCoshen—to decide our strategy. I wanted to veto the entire budget. No one had ever done this before, and we weren't sure what would happen if I did. I was concerned but willing to break new ground on this issue. We were at a critical crossroads. Four years earlier, we had started down a new road of lower taxes and less government. Now the Democrats were trying to take us back.

On Sunday, I scheduled an interview with the state's largest morning newspaper. I said I would veto the entire budget if it passed the Democrat-controlled legislature. After my announcement, the Democrats backed away from some of their proposals. I had raised the stakes, drawn a line in the sand, and many of them didn't want to cross it. However, the battle was not over yet. The legislature pared approximately $200 million off Kunicki's original proposal, but the budget they presented to me still had more than $500 million in new taxes.

By this time, the legislature knew how I used the veto power. Applying their best cryptographic skills, they crafted what they thought was a veto-proof package. The tax increases were woven into various parts of the budget in such a way that made it very difficult to isolate and veto them without vetoing other things I supported. We spent two weeks just trying to figure out how everything fit together. Once we unraveled the pieces, we repeated the process of walking through every change the legislature had made to my budget and deciding our veto strategy.

Legislators and others began making appointments with me, petitioning me not to veto certain spending programs. Sometimes, when they wouldn't take no for an answer, I held up a sign on my desk that reads, "What part of 'no' don't you understand?" By now, the giant pencil Cloyd Porter had given me was a mere stub. So he went back to the Burlington Lumber Yard and returned with a new pencil ten feet long. When his aides were delivering it to my office (it took two of them to carry it), they were spotted by some Democrat legislative staff. The drama started to build inside the capitol. Nervous Democrats wondered how I would extricate myself from the "veto-proof" box they had constructed. And the media continued to speculate that I might veto the entire budget and throw government into chaos. Predictions of doom and gloom were rampant. Chicken Littles lined the halls.

On August 8, 1991, we scheduled a press conference in the capitol rotunda. After four weeks of intensive review, I was ready to submit my vetoes to the legislature. In my remarks to the legislature and the media, I said, "This is not the time to abandon the policies that have worked so well and succumb to the temptation for a quick fix to deal with spending demands. . . . The importance of continued restraint in overall state taxing and spending cannot be overemphasized."

The budget I had submitted to the legislature back in February was balanced, without tax increases. The budget I received from the legislature on July 3 contained $535 million in tax increases and higher spending. On August 8, I signed a balanced budget that held state spending increases to the rate of inflation and contained no tax increases. Gone was the higher spending. Gone was the $535 million tax increase. I used the veto an unprecedented 457 times. The list of vetoes I sent back to the legislature was 211 pages long.

ROBBING PETER TO PAY PAUL

In my 1991 budget, I fulfilled my 1987 campaign promise to increase the state share of school funding to 50 percent. And yet, without controls on local school spending, property taxes were not going down—in fact, they were still going up by 8 and 10 percent a year. Clearly, without cost controls, there was virtually no correlation between increased state aid and lower property taxes. By 1993, I had increased state aid to local schools by more than $1 billion, but the schools were spending the extra money *and* getting more from property taxes at the local level. Over a ten-year period, school spending had increased by 105 percent, while enrollment had grown by only 6 percent.

Year after year, I had reintroduced caps on school spending, and the legislature shot them down every time. I kept trying, but up against a very powerful education establishment that had a vested interest in more spending, I couldn't get the public to understand that controlling school spending was the key to controlling property taxes. As my proposals worked their way through the legislative process, they always seemed to become muddied by exceptions, exemptions, and exclusions. People wanted lower property taxes; they didn't want confusing formulas.

In 1993, we came up with a new idea. I simply proposed a freeze on property tax rates. "Freeze" was something everyone understood. People knew property taxes were out of control, and the freeze spoke to their concern. To most people, it meant, "We're going to stop this thing in its tracks." It didn't take long for the discussion over property taxes to shift. Finally, people in the Main Street cafe began to understand that to hold these taxes where they were, spending had to be "frozen" as well.

Despite growing public support, my rate freeze was headed nowhere in the legislature. Because they still held control of both houses, the Democrats could bottle up my proposals in committee. Then one day, I was approached by Senator Marv Roshell, a conservative Democrat from Chippewa Falls who had supported many of my welfare and budget initiatives. He was tired of the senate and was interested in a job in my administration. The composition of the senate at the time was sixteen Democrats and fifteen Republicans. If Marv left, it would be deadlocked at 15–15. I appointed him to a position in the state Department of Labor. His seat, and two others that had become vacant, needed to be filled in the special elections in April. All three seats had been held by Democrats. (Russ Feingold had been elected to the U.S. Senate and Tom Barrett to the U.S. House of Representatives.)

The rate freeze became a major issue. It allowed us to circumvent the bureaucrats and interest groups and speak directly to the people about the need to control spending. Even the Democrat candidates began aligning themselves with the freeze. However, it was clearly our proposal, and Republican candidates who supported it won two of the three seats. For the first time in my seven years as governor, one house of the legislature was controlled by my own party.

This changed everything. It was now impossible for Democrats to bury my proposals in committee and prevent a vote on the floor of at least one house. And if I could win approval of key initiatives in the senate, the assembly Democrats would at least have to come to the table at a conference committee and compromise. Before, my only real weapon was the veto—and that only worked if the legislature passed something close enough to what I had proposed. Now I had an offensive weapon in the legislative process itself.

The senate didn't waste any time passing school spending

controls, and the assembly Democrats were obliged to negotiate in conference committee. With an election approaching and strong support among voters for a freeze on spending, they agreed to most of what the senate had passed. On August 10, 1993, I finally signed school spending controls into law. Under the new law, school districts throughout the state were limited to annual per pupil spending increases of no more than the rate of inflation. This was a reasonable policy, consistent with the philosophy I had fought for with school choice—that a quality education can be had at a reasonable price.

Having lost on spending controls, and with the 1994 gubernatorial and legislative races approaching, the Democrats needed something dramatic to capture public sentiment on the issue. The press had been touting Governor John Engler's plan in our neighbor state of Michigan to shift almost all education funding from the local districts to the state. But to pay for the shift, Michigan was increasing other state taxes. Emboldened by this approach, Wisconsin Democrats introduced legislation to remove school spending from the property tax completely and fund it entirely at the state level. Although they wouldn't admit it publicly, they knew it would be necessary to increase some taxes to pay for this shift, just as Michigan was doing.

Reporters quickly descended on my capitol office, "camping out," as they are known to do, to get a quick reaction from me. As I was making my way through a small corridor between my office and the bathroom, a reporter cornered me and asked me what I thought. In one of my more candid responses as governor, I called the proposal "idiotic." To fully fund local education at the state level would have required doubling the income tax or doubling the sales tax. Wisconsin's economy was producing jobs at nearly double the national rate. I didn't want a tax increase to jeopardize that. My comments were widely carried by the press. I think the Democrats figured they had us on the run, because now we appeared to the public to be "against" cutting property taxes.

Bill McCoshen, my chief of staff, together with Christopher

Mohrman, my top budget staffer, and Rick Chandler, began a series of discussions with Mike Ellis, the Republican majority leader of the senate, and David Prosser, the Republican minority leader of the assembly. We agreed a tax increase was unwise, and without it, the state could not assume all local school spending. Besides, local school boards felt it was important to retain some funding at the local level. I agreed. Education is best handled at the local level. If the state picked up all the funding, local control would erode. The last thing I wanted was the state government running local schools.

Sensing the kill on this politically charged issue, the assembly passed its proposal to shift all local school funding to the state. The senate passed a bill more in line with my original budget— providing for increased state aid to local schools and spending controls, which lowered the property tax burden at the local level.

The two bills were brought to conference committee so that a compromise could be worked out. Both sides gave a little, and in the end agreed to a plan removing two-thirds of school spending from the property tax. This meant the state government had to pick up $1.2 billion in new spending in the next budget and simultaneously reduce school funding from property taxes by 25 percent.

Rick Chandler was worried that this would force a tax increase. I understood the challenge differently, because I saw it as a tool to control government spending even more than we had, in ways that I know would never have worked without the pressure of the $1.2 billion tax cut on the books. When I signed the property tax cut into law, I promised I would find the new money without raising sales or income tax rates. "All state agencies are going to have to tighten their belts," I said. "I'm going to put state government on a Slim Fast diet immediately this summer. . . . Schools are now going to get first priority. Everybody else is in second place."

How to pay for the property tax cut—the largest tax cut in state history—became a central issue during my 1994 campaign for a third term as governor. My opponent proposed sales and income tax increases to pay for a full-scale shifting of school funding to the state. "Government would just be picking a different pocket," I said. Merely shifting one tax for another inevitably leads to a higher overall tax burden on everyone.

The history of prior property tax cut efforts in Wisconsin demonstrated that "robbing Peter to pay Paul" has never lowered either Peter or Paul's taxes. In 1911, Wisconsin Governor Francis E. McGovern proposed the state's first income tax as a remedy to reduce property taxes. In doing so he said that "this legislation should come to the taxpayer . . . not in the form of an additional burden, but in lieu of other taxes now found to be unsatisfactory." In 1961, Governor Gaylord Nelson imposed a state sales tax to reduce property taxes. He said that "this measure earmarks for real property tax relief all revenues raised by the special taxes on consumer purchases." Over time, however, such new taxes earmarked for property tax relief just didn't work. When government increases taxes, it *always* finds new ways to spend the money. The only solution is to cut spending.

During the campaign, I continued to promise that I would "fund" property tax cuts without raising other tax rates. The "experts" once again pronounced this impossible. Some even suggested I was being "disingenuous" with the public for saying I could do it. This was reminiscent of the "experts" who said I couldn't balance the budget in 1987, 1989, or 1991 without raising taxes. The voters made up their own minds. I'm still here. The state senate remained under Republican control, and the state assembly switched from a Democrat to a Republican majority. For the first time in twenty-four years, Republicans controlled both houses of the state legislature.

Absorbing $1.2 billion in new spending in a budget that had previously been $16 billion, without raising taxes, was not an easy task. It's the equivalent of the federal government assuming the spending obligations of seven states the size of Wisconsin without raising federal taxes or increasing the deficit. Again, we began the process by asking all state agencies to submit budgets with 5 percent cuts, applying the model we had set up in 1987 and followed each year. Because we had to come up with more cuts than usual, I asked my agency heads to submit cuts of 5 percent in the first year and 10 percent in the second.

We looked at the savings this model brought us. I made department heads go back to their staffs time after time. We were getting closer but not close enough. We needed to be even bolder—to reprogram how much government was spending, we had to reformulate government.

In effect, we had been handed this opportunity, and I wasn't going to let it slip away. Agency heads and DOA budget analysts weren't just crunching numbers, they were thinking, putting their heads together. No one likes to be told, "You can't," or "It's impossible." People told Frank Lloyd Wright, one of Wisconsin's great talents, that he couldn't build his buildings. But from his hillside home and studio, Taliesin, about forty miles west of Madison, Wright created architecture that changed the way America lived. Now I was in a room overlooking the construction of Madison's new Frank Lloyd Wright convention center, and working, really, to change how Wisconsin was governed.

I wanted to be away from the phone and other distractions to focus entirely on what we were about to do. From December 1 to January 18 we met in a conference room at the DOA, two blocks from my capitol office, to come up with the cuts we needed to fund property tax relief. On twenty-seven separate days we gathered around a large Frank Lloyd Wright–inspired table in the DOA conference room. Secretary Klauser never let anyone eat on it. One night I ordered pizza for the budget analysts, and they all sat around the table sheepishly eating their pizza while Klauser glared at them so they wouldn't spill anything on the table. During these sessions, I constantly challenged the analysts to go "outside the box" of conventional thinking to come up with new approaches to operating government. I kept pushing and saying to them, "Anything is possible, this is the time to do it."

When I finally unveiled the budget in a speech before the state legislature, I said,

> [This budget] is the culmination of eight years of hard work and innovation. It is the final step in a long-fought battle for property tax relief. Everybody said we couldn't do it. Everybody said we couldn't take $1 billion off the property tax without raising the sales [and] income tax. And I am here today to tell you that we did it. When I traveled around the state last fall, I told the people of Wisconsin that the state would assume two-thirds of school costs. We did. I told them we would do this without a general tax increase. We did.
>
> We have never spent more time putting a budget together—literally thousands of hours combing through agency budgets line by line. Looking for efficiencies. Looking for programs and positions that are no longer fundamental to our state responsibilities. As I said, it wasn't easy. But this budget is straightforward . . . It turns a tremendous challenge into a tremendous opportunity. And it provides the largest single tax cut in the history of this state.

The 1995 budget, funding state government over a two-year period, represented the first time in state history that property taxes were cut without increasing other tax rates. It was a balanced budget, paying for tax cuts by reducing government spending and using higher revenues flowing into the state treasury from Wisconsin's strong economy. The bulk of the spending cuts came from reducing the budgets of state agencies, but part of it also flowed from an unprecedented reorganization of state government, restructuring twenty-one agencies, eliminating twelve others, and phasing out 170 government boards and commissions.

In addition to funding the tax cut, the budget continued to fund other obligations the state had made in prior budgets. These included increased funding for local governments, prisons, prosecutors, courts, and certain state employees. This spending, as well as part of the funding for the tax cut, was possible because of $400 million in higher revenues the state was receiving due to economic growth. The tax cuts we had achieved years earlier were helping spur economic growth that in turn was helping fund another major tax cut for the people of Wisconsin. In every budget since 1987, I had either proposed tax cuts or vetoed tax increases passed by the legislature. It hadn't been easy, but now it was paying off.

The last decade of balancing budgets in Wisconsin shows that effective government does not require deficit spending. Government can provide necessary services to its citizens without spending more than it takes in. We have reformed welfare, improved education, created jobs, protected the environment, beefed up law enforcement, and cut taxes without creating a deficit.

Budgets can be balanced without cutting spending to the bone. Overall, state spending has increased during the past decade in Wisconsin, but less than in the past, and never more than incoming revenues.

Discipline really is the heart of the matter when it comes to balancing budgets. And discipline requires leadership. Excessive tax-and-spend policies of government can be changed, but it isn't easy. I had to fight major battles with my budget and use the veto to make it happen. It was and is a constant struggle. There is so much political and bureaucratic weight pushing for more spending that it takes continuous pressure and a willingness to fight to change it.

But my experience—and the experiences of other governors—demonstrates that the culture of government spending can be changed. Leaders who have the guts to do what is necessary and take the flak can withstand—and even prosper from—the political assault of special interests trying to block change. We had a good plan, and we stuck to our guns. We've been able to accomplish our objectives of lowering taxes and increasing efficiency. We have a government that provides important services but takes less out of the pockets of hard-working people.

We've accomplished at the state level what still seems impossible on the national front: reducing the size and scope of a federal government that has built itself up over the past century does not happen overnight. But it will start with returning more power and authority to the states, where balancing budgets is not an empty promise, but a way of life.

CHAPTER SIX

JOBS FOR THE NEXT CENTURY

I am a pro-business governor. It's not a Republican stance or a Democrat stance, it's simply what makes sense to me. *Pro-business* to me means "pro-jobs," and I don't see how government can be pro-jobs while being hostile to the businesses that create them, and I don't think there is anything more important than having a good job. Jobs are how people buy their own homes, send their children to college, and realize a better life. Having a good job and working hard to support yourself and your family is the bedrock of a strong society. America's work ethic is one of the core values that has made our culture so strong. I grew up in a small community that, like a lot of towns across Wisconsin and America, was a patchwork of small businesses. I never worked for a large corporation, and I didn't know many people who did. These small businesses create most of the jobs in America and keep our work ethic alive.

Former British prime minister Margaret Thatcher once wrote that "there is no better course for understanding free-market economics than life in a corner shop." That was the "pro-business" environment I grew up with. It wasn't some abstract notion of capitalism. It was my father's grocery store, and the hardware store down the street, and the local bank. It was my family and our friends and neighbors working hard, selling a good product, and making a profit so they could create more jobs for others and take care of their own families.

My strong belief in the value of work comes from my own upbringing. In my family, going to work was right up there with going to church. It was a moral issue. Being a good Catholic meant following the Ten Commandments, going to confession when you sinned, and working your tail off. So I started working in the grocery store when I was six, and when I was twelve, my father put me to work painting barns during the summer. I had to climb makeshift ladders and hang from precarious heights to get those barns painted. If only the federal government had been on the job in those days. The Department of Labor and the Occupational Safety and Health Administration certainly would have shut down my father's barn-painting business for safety and child labor violations. As much as I yearned to do other things with my summers, the experience made me appreciate the opportunity of having a job.

I was actually fired from my first "real" job. To get a summer job working highway construction, you were supposed to be eighteen. I was only seventeen, and I lied about my age, but my father helped me get the job and didn't have a problem with my fib. As I said, working was a moral issue in my family.

I shoveled asphalt onto the road bed for the machines to pack down. The company loved me because I worked so hard. Almost two months went by before my true age was discovered. We were doing a job near Elroy, and because Elroy was a close-knit community, someone let the foreman know I wasn't yet eighteen. I was promptly dispatched from the road crew and back to the grocery store. I reapplied the next summer when I really was eighteen, and the construction company hired me back as a blacktop shoveler. I worked for the company again in the summer while I was in college, and even though I weighed in at a mere 150 pounds, I became valued for my jackhammer skills.

Once they put it in my hands, they knew I would hammer away all day long like nobody else. It is a lot like being a governor.

Outside Wisconsin, I'm known best for welfare reform and education vouchers, but promoting economic growth was my first and most important goal. I hammered away at it constantly during my first campaign, in my next two campaigns, and in most of the speeches I've given in a decade as governor. No other issue has received more of my attention. I've done this because I believe promoting economic growth is one of the most important things government can do. In my 1986 campaign for governor I said that "the *primary objective* of the Wisconsin state government will be to enhance opportunities for prosperity for the citizens of this state. Simply put, that means more and better jobs."

Political insiders told me I could never win being "pro-business" in an "anti-business" state. "No one has ever been elected running openly as a pro-business candidate here," they said. Wisconsin was the birthplace of the Progressive movement, the people who brought down big-business monopolies. "Tone it down," they said. "Just let businesses know privately that you're on their side."

After twenty years in the state legislature, I knew a fair amount about politics, but I have to admit I didn't understand this. Had we become so locked into labels that being pro-business was a bad thing? Jobs are good for people; businesses create and sustain jobs. Isn't that common sense?

When I first ran for governor, Wisconsin's economy was in the tank. We had lost 23 percent of our manufacturing jobs between 1979 and 1983, and our economic growth rate was one-half the national average. We ranked fortieth among all states in nonagricultural job creation. But we had shown real strength in creating jobs in one category: between 1979 and 1985, government jobs in Wisconsin increased by 3.8 percent.

I believe that in their hearts, Governor Tony Earl and his Democrat supporters in the legislature wanted to create jobs for

the people of Wisconsin. They cared as much about the working class as anybody. I just think they were locked on a path
that had begun fifty years before with the New Deal. In their
minds, the need to rescue workers from a crumbling economy
had evolved into a Doberman pinscher–like need to protect
workers from business—business that couldn't be trusted. And
this attitude translated into action. The state government was
basically in an adversarial relationship with the businesses of
our state. Government was so entrenched in regulating businesses and trying to prevent them from leaving or downsizing
that it never devoted any serious energy to recruiting or
expanding businesses. Governor Earl assigned commissions to
study the problems, but when it came right down to it, he was
focusing his energies on issues like "comparable worth" legislation. I'm not opposed to fairness in the workplace, but I think
it's fair to say that where you direct your energies is a pretty
good indication of what your attitude is.

It wasn't working. People were fed up. A group of
Wisconsin business leaders formed an organization called the
"bow wow society" to publicize the state's anti-business policies.
They placed advertisements in the *Wall Street Journal* and other
publications, warning companies to stay away from Wisconsin.
The official state slogan at the time, the one used to attract vis-
itors and tourists, was "Escape to Wisconsin." The bow wow
society's slogan was "Escape Wisconsin." A common quip
among business people was, "Would the last company to leave
Wisconsin please turn out the lights?" Governor Jim Thompson, from the neighboring state of Illinois, placed billboards on
the border saying, "Come to Illinois: Land of Better Business."
And Wisconsin companies were doing it, taking jobs out of the
state and killing the dreams of working people. Ironically, as our
businesses moved to Illinois, welfare recipients were moving our
way across the border to take advantage of Wisconsin's higher
welfare benefits. Conservative Democrats in blue-collar towns
like Kenosha, Racine, and Beloit were really upset by this.

Before I became governor, one of the state's largest employers, the Kimberly Clark Corporation, moved its headquarters out of the state. Kimberly Clark chairman Darwin Smith publicly cited the state government's anti-business policies as the reason for the move. Tony Earl disputed the notion that state government was hostile to business, but Smith offered to prove it by helping to pay for a study examining state government's policies toward business. The governor agreed and established the Wisconsin Strategic Development Commission to examine the issue.

As minority leader of the state assembly, I was appointed to serve on the twenty-two-member commission. We examined all aspects of government activity that affect business development, and although the bipartisan commission couldn't come out and say it, Darwin Smith was right. The commission recommended a comprehensive change in state policies, including improving the state's transportation system, enhancing state business development programs, and changing state government's high tax and spending policies.

Although the commission issued its report on August 1, 1985, and the governor began implementing some of its recommendations before the 1986 election, it was too little too late. In his first three years as governor, working in partnership with businesses to create more jobs had not been a priority, and it still was not something he strongly believed in. I made it clear during the campaign that I would use state government to actively promote private sector job creation. I told voters I believed that the state "should focus on creating jobs and income." And I promised I would play a hands-on role in making it happen.

In my first major policy address as governor, I told the legislature and citizens of Wisconsin, "Our biggest challenge is to create more jobs in Wisconsin." And I added, "To make our state a leader in business and job creation *we must change attitudes. Our own and especially the attitudes that others have about Wisconsin.*"

I was willing to do or try almost anything to bring jobs and people back to Wisconsin. So many of the changes I proposed—from cutting taxes to welfare reform—were intrinsically part of this drive. I made it clear to everyone that I wanted to make government a partner rather than an obstacle to businesses. The first bill I signed into law increased state funding for state tourism promotion. When I was campaigning for governor I went to towns in the northern part of the state that governors rarely went to. It's one of the most beautiful parts of the state— well off the beaten path. Many of the people who lived there depended on tourism dollars to make a living. They felt no one "down south in Madison" cared about them. After I was elected I invited a group of them from different towns around the state—men and women who ran little motels, bait shops, and restaurants—to help come up with recommendations for my first budget. In my 1987 budget, I increased state funding for tourism promotion by 300 percent. In the past decade, I've increased the tourism promotion budget by more than 600 percent and established a separate state Department of Tourism. It is an example of government spending that pays off in the long run. Wisconsin's tourism industry has created almost 50,000 new jobs since 1986. The investment of $8 million in promotion has helped increase annual tourist spending by $1.38 billion. That spending, and the new jobs it creates, has generated more than $400 million in tax revenues to state and local government. That's almost a 5,000 percent return on the initial investment.

When I was crisscrossing the state during the campaign with my friend and driver, John Tries, I listened to ideas from a lot of people. Over those few months, I was so impressed with the ideas I heard from people who weren't in government that I promised myself I would bring in outsiders to run government. Bruno Mauer, president of the Tool Service Corporation in Milwaukee, had been a frequent and vocal critic of the state's anti-business policy. He had testified at legislative hearings about how hard it was to do business in Wisconsin. I placed a call to him a week before the election and said, "Bruno, if I win this election, I want you to be my secretary of development." He was not impressed. "Why on earth would I want to go work for the government?" he said. "I've got a business to run." I told him to think about it and that I'd be back in touch.

The night before the election, I called him again. "Bruno, I'm going to win this thing, and when I do I'm going to call you and offer you the job." He was unmoved. "You haven't won it yet, Tommy," he said. The day after I won I called him and offered him the job, and he took it, but on the condition that he would stay only one year (he stayed for three).

It didn't take us long to realize we had our own brand of "government sense" that needed to be replaced in Wisconsin. In his first meeting with the one hundred or so civil servants in his department, Bruno was met with coolness, and even hostility. One career employee stood up and questioned Bruno's "qualifications" for the job. "How can you run this department?" the bureaucrat said. "You've never worked for government and you don't know how we do things." That was exactly the point. It spoke volumes about the attitude in state government we wanted to change.

Bruno and I realized that after the election we had a small window of opportunity to make major changes. I wanted to shake up the system right away, to let people know we were serious. The tax cuts I was proposing in my budget would be part of the strategy. They would demonstrate that we were serious about making the state a good place to do business. We also immediately began overhauling the Department of Development. Its very existence meant the state already had made an institutional commitment to help businesses create jobs, but it was a backwater department with little focus or resources. I made it one of my strongest agencies. In my first budget I increased its funding and consolidated state government's business development activities in the department. I made my intentions very clear, telling the legislature and the public that my goal was to "make government responsive to business needs and insure that government contacts with business are positive, helpful and efficient." I said the beefed-up department would "aggressively promote business recruitment and expansion, and improve relations between government and private businesses." By and large, the public and the state legislature agreed. It was amazing, really, in a state that was supposed to be so anti-business. So much for labels.

What had been a hodgepodge of different Band-Aid programs became a single development fund with the sole mission of retaining existing jobs and helping businesses create new ones. We increased funding for the development fund from $2 million to $20 million, and introduced new flexibility into the system, so we could be more responsive to the specific needs of individual developing businesses. This allowed me to listen to what a particular company was facing, and then tailor an assistance package that directly met its main concerns. We replaced a highly bureaucratic process with case-by-case common sense. We did not engage in loud bidding wars to attract giant automakers to Wisconsin; we worked with individual companies to remove barriers to expansion and job creation.

Soon after I was elected, a major food distribution company in La Crosse came to us with a problem. It was trying to build a new corporate headquarters to house its expanded operations in the state. Part of the land it wanted to build on had a large hole filled with old tires and garbage next to a railroad track. The company wanted to remove the debris and put in a pond as part of its landscaping plan. This required permits from the state Department of Natural Resources (DNR).

Under orders from the federal Fish and Wildlife Service, DNR refused the permits. The land—complete with its railroad track and dump pile—was officially considered a backwater of the Mississippi. Under federal rules, it had to stay the way it was. The company had gotten nowhere trying to reason with

DNR and federal officials. By the time I got involved, the company chairman was ready to move the business out of the state. We sat down with DNR and worked with federal officials to try to solve the problem. We brought them all together to the site so they could examine it. When they actually saw it, they changed their minds and allowed the company to build and clean up the garbage. Because we took the time to bring various government agencies together, several hundred people in La Crosse kept their jobs. And since then, the company has built more distribution centers in other parts of the state, creating more jobs for people. The chairman of the company—who had "hated" state government and was ready to move the company's jobs out of the state—became an ally who helped us attract other businesses to Wisconsin. That is what a pro-business government can do.

Before I was elected, American Motors Corporation (AMC) announced it would eliminate 5,500 jobs in Wisconsin by shutting down its assembly line and engine plant in Kenosha. (It was the same plant where I had applied for a job after high school.) The December before I took office, we thought we had staved off the shut-down by reaching an agreement to help the company build a new plant and retrain its workers.

Chrysler Corporation then purchased AMC, and we began working with them to keep the plant running. I spoke with then–chairman Lee Iacocca and was given what I thought was his word that the company would keep the operation running. Then in January 1988, Chrysler suddenly changed its mind—it was pulling out. Instead of sulking, I started working to try to save those jobs. The labor unions wanted us to file suit and try to force Chrysler to stay, but I decided the best course was to negotiate with the company. I believed a lawsuit would be viewed as too confrontational and would likely cause the company to pull its entire operation out of Kenosha. We would end up with nothing but a vacant plant. Bruno Mauer, Jim Klauser, and I worked into the summer trying to save at least part of the operation. These were the toughest negotiations I have ever been involved in. Eventually, Chrysler agreed to keep the engine plant open with more than 1,000 jobs. Chrysler still runs the engine plant in Kenosha, and it is one of the company's most profitable, thanks in large part to the hard work and dedication of its union workers. In 1995, Chrysler announced a $350 million expansion of the site, and more new jobs.

In 1988, Chrysler was making changes to become a stronger company. One step it was taking was shutting down outdated assembly lines. I worked with labor and business and local government to save what made sense, but I didn't focus all our energy on saving jobs at a company that was trying to remain competitive, or on forcing the company to stay. Instead, I put a lot of time and effort into creating a pro-business environment in Kenosha and working to help new businesses take advantage of it. From our experience with Chrysler, we learned that Kenosha and southeastern Wisconsin needed to diversify its economy—too many jobs were dependent on a few major employers. If a large company like Chrysler downsized, the entire local economy was vulnerable. As it turned out, the last piece of legislation I had worked to pass as a legislator before I became governor—a deregulation bill that allowed utility companies to diversify—helped us accomplish our goal of strengthening Kenosha's economy.

A Wisconsin power company owned a large tract of land in the area next to one of its power plants and began developing it into a business park. We began helping the community aggressively market the industrial park, which led to a tip that Rust-Oleum, a major paint manufacturer based in Illinois, was looking for a place to expand. I immediately flew to Illinois to meet with Rust-Oleum's chairman. He had never had a governor go to him personally to discuss job creation. After several meetings, Rust-Oleum agreed to be the first company to move in. Although my persistence no doubt played an important role in convincing Rust-Oleum to move to Wisconsin, there were other reasons as well. One was the company's interest in chemistry research for its products. When we learned this was an important issue, we introduced company representatives to officials at the University of Wisconsin, who agreed to help them with research. By putting in the effort and bringing people together to solve practical issues, we spurred the creation of jobs for workers in Wisconsin. The industrial park today is home to forty-two small and medium-size companies. Kenosha's unemployment rate is well below the national average, and the city has been featured in such national publications as *Business Week* as a rags-to-riches success story.

I have continually used the bully pulpit of the governor's office to promote Wisconsin as a good place to do business. It meant constantly saying that I was "pro-business," and so was Wisconsin. And it wasn't enough just to say it. I had to demonstrate it. So I threw myself into projects like expanding export opportunities for state businesses. I led fourteen trade missions to twenty foreign countries. I took business people along—most of them ran small businesses that had a good product, but they couldn't afford to market their products to countries that wanted them. I took Christmas tree growers to Mexico, and they landed several new contracts. I took ginseng farmers to Asia, and today we're the number one state in ginseng exports to Asia.

Having a governor along on a trade mission means a lot to the head of a small company. Foreign heads of state actually treat governors as if we're important. It opens doors. Since we started helping companies export their products, exports from the state have grown at a pace nearly triple the national rate. And export-related jobs in the state have increased from 66,000 in 1987 to 200,000 in 1995.

Wisconsin's liberal intellectuals were offended at what they sniffingly refer to as my constant "cheerleading" on behalf of the state to try to attract more jobs and businesses. They thought this sort of constant promotion somehow demeaned the office of the governor. Governors, after all, have staffs to do this sort of thing. Perhaps the liberals were arrogant in their belief that they were the party of the working class. It was as if they couldn't understand that someone on the other side of the political spectrum could be creative and innovative, as if this were somehow their monopoly. They were overlooking something very important: to be the party of the working class, you have to work with business to create jobs for working people.

I doubt if anything jolted the Wisconsin Democrat politicians as much as the endorsements I received when I ran for a third term in 1994—from six labor unions. On Labor Day, my campaign ran a television ad across the state featuring John Budzinski of the Steamfitters Union of Milwaukee. He was a no-nonsense workingman, and his words, "It's all about jobs, and Tommy keeps 'em coming," could not be ignored. I am a pro-business governor. And a pro-union governor. And a pro-worker governor. Since 1986, our economy has produced more than 530,000 new jobs and more high-paying manufacturing jobs than any other state. So much for labels.

Hardly a day goes by that I'm not on the phone or meeting with some business person about creating more jobs in Wisconsin. I never came to grips with the fact that the Kimberly Clark Corporation had left. It was a constant reminder of Wisconsin's anti-business attitudes in the early 1980s. After I became governor I started calling Kimberly Clark CEO Wayne Sanders on a regular basis. I was very persistent. If the company wasn't going to move back, maybe it would consider Wisconsin for future expansions. In 1991, my persistence paid off. Kimberly Clark built a brand-new facility in Neenah, Wisconsin, offering three hundred new jobs. At the press conference, Wayne Sanders said Wisconsin is now "the best place in America to do business." What does that mean? It means more and better jobs for real people. Today, Kimberly Clark employs 6,800 people in Wisconsin—1,600 more people than it employed when it announced it would leave Wisconsin in

1984. That's 1,600 families who now have real, tangible opportunities that weren't there before.

It took more than my phone calls and "cheerleading" to convince companies to create more jobs in Wisconsin. It took hundreds of dedicated employees in state government who worked hard at it every day. But it couldn't have happened without changing the policies of state government at a broader level. Business is measured against the bottom line. Jobs are created when businesses make profits. Government policies—from education to welfare, from criminal justice to environmental protection—have a direct impact on profits and the bottom line.

If government had done so much to make jobs and businesses leave the state, certainly it could do as much to help bring them back. High taxes were a major reason businesses, jobs, and people were leaving the state. Businesses are like customers at a grocery store. They pay a certain price to government—primarily in taxes and regulation—to do business in a particular location. The "product" they are buying is the quality of the workforce, good infrastructure, schools, low crime rates, and other tangible and intangible characteristics of a location that will help make the business profitable. Wisconsin had many of those attributes, including an exceptional workforce with a superior work ethic. But our prices were too high. Companies simply were taking their business elsewhere.

I proposed a series of tax changes my first year in office, including continuing the 60 percent exclusion of capital gains from taxation. I told the legislature, "This 60 percent exclusion will attract more entrepreneurs into Wisconsin who will start businesses that will employ more and more people. It will also encourage entrepreneurs already here to expand and provide even more jobs."

This is a debate Washington has had for years, and like the Democrats in Washington, the Democrats in Wisconsin said no. They dusted off their tried-and-true class warfare rhetoric. "A tax break for the rich," they pronounced. Yet a survey of the

Wisconsin tax code showed that 80 percent of the people with capital gains had incomes below $50,000. It didn't have anything to do with CEOs or Wall Street. Most of the people with capital gains were the farmers selling livestock or the plumber selling his business and retiring. They would benefit the most, as would small business owners like my father, and risk-taking entrepreneurs who would create most of the new jobs. So when the legislature reduced the capital gains exclusion, I vetoed its change and restored the original exclusion. And when the legislature reduced the exclusion again in 1991, I vetoed that as well.

Today, Wisconsin is one of only a handful of states to exclude a portion of capital gains from taxation. That is one reason Wisconsin's entrepreneurial climate is now rated the best in the Midwest and the tenth best in the nation by Cognetics, a Cambridge, Massachusetts, business research firm. We have large manufacturers like Harley-Davidson in Milwaukee, but our manufacturing base is primarily small businesses. While the nation has lost nearly 600,000 manufacturing jobs in the past decade, Wisconsin businesses have created more than 86,000 new ones. We're a medium-sized state, but we're number one in manufacturing job growth, and we rank fourth in the nation in the percentage of manufacturing jobs in our workforce. Excluding 60 percent of capital gains taxation means a lot to a small manufacturing firm. It is an important arrow in my quiver when I talk to businesses about creating more jobs in Wisconsin. Eliminating or reducing the capital gains tax at the federal level would generate economic growth in America just as it has in Wisconsin. If only Washington could extricate itself from its "label locks."

As a result of capital gains tax cuts combined with other tax reductions over the past decade, Wisconsin now has one of the lowest business tax burdens in the nation. Our state business climate rating, according to the national accounting firm Grant-Thornton, climbed from a national ranking of thirty-seventh in 1987 to fourteenth in 1988, eighth in 1989, and third in 1990. We've worked to lower other bottom-line business costs, like unemployment compensation and workers compensation. When I started as governor, our unemployment compensation program was broke. Employers pay into the unemployment compensation fund to compensate workers if they lose their jobs. Because business was so bad, and companies were leaving, people were being laid off. We had exhausted all the money in the fund. In fact, we had been in debt to the federal government to the tune of $500 million. By bringing businesses back into the state, we've been able to lower the unemployment compensation tax on employers three times, and today, the fund has a surplus of $1.5 billion.

The same thing happened with workers compensation costs. We have kept workers compensation rates low, and that has helped make starting and running a business in Wisconsin more attractive. In 1995, workers compensation rates in Wisconsin declined by 11.9 percent, saving businesses more than $135 million in insurance premiums over twelve months. The National Council on Compensation Insurance calls Wisconsin's workers compensation a "model for a well-functioning" program. These sorts of nuts-and-bolts changes are not headline-grabbers, but they make a big difference on the bottom line.

We also invested in government programs that help businesses start and expand, like increased state funding for highway construction (as the 1985 Strategic Development Commission had recommended). We started a major new road-building program to ensure that every part of the state would have easy access to our interstate highway system. We also more than doubled state aid for local airport improvements and upgrades. Why? Because good transportation is an important bottom-line issue to businesses wanting to create more jobs. And we created new programs like Transportation Economic Development Grants, which provide state funds to local communities for transportation improvements directly tied to the creation or retention of jobs in the community. Since we started the program in 1987, 126 grants have gone to 104 Wisconsin communities to create or retain private sector jobs for 33,563 workers in those communities.

REAL-WORLD RESULTS

By the end of my first four years, Wisconsin's economy had turned around. We had controlled government spending, cut taxes, and created a pro-business government. The private sector responded, creating 250,000 new jobs. More people now were moving into the state than were leaving. We ranked third among all fifty states in the creation of high-paying manufacturing jobs, and business starts were up 10.2 percent compared to a nationwide decline of 1.1 percent. Our unemployment rate, which had exceeded the national rate in 1987, now was the sixth lowest in the nation.

When the recession hit the country's economy in 1991 and 1992, Wisconsin's economy kept growing. We were no longer the "rust belt." (And now, we even had Rust-Oleum.) Wisconsin avoided the brunt of the recession in 1991 and 1992. We started to see that our commitment to controlling taxes and spending—and the pro-business policies we had implemented over four years—were making a difference in people's lives. While other states were raising sales and income taxes to meet budget deficits due to the nationwide economic slowdown, revenues to Wisconsin state government continued to grow because of economic growth. In my 1991 State of the State speech, I made it very clear I would continue with those policies during my next term as governor. Individual income tax *collections* had increased by 8.8 percent from the previous year—not by raising tax rates, but through economic growth. While most of the nation headed for the pit of recession, Wisconsin revenue collections were stronger than predicted, and our state was one of only three states east of the Mississippi to close its books with a budget surplus. We had watched other states hike taxes to support increased state spending, and their economies were stumbling. As a result, many of those states were facing another budget shortfall and another round of tax increases.

Despite a strong state economy, not all the businesses in Wisconsin survived the national recession. The biggest blow came in Eau Claire, in the northwestern part of the state. Uniroyal decided to shut down its tire plant there, throwing 650 people out of work. Democrats in the state legislature immediately pounced on this human suffering, calling it the result of my "soft" approach toward businesses. Their adversarial instinct reemerged. To liberal Democrats, the traditional way to protect workers threatened by plant closings during a recession was to toughen the plant closing laws, to try to prevent the plants from closing. When I resisted, they called me "anti-worker." I thought the best thing to do was to give the company every reason to stay open. I spent hours negotiating, but to no avail. Still, I thought, wasn't it better to provide state funds to retrain workers and make concerted efforts to bring businesses to Eau Claire?

There were many small successes, but the major payoff came in March 1995, when Hutchinson Technology agreed to open a new plant in Eau Claire with 1,400 well-paying jobs. And later in 1995, this leading manufacturer of computer components announced it was adding another 1,000 jobs in Eau Claire. It had taken time, money, and effort, but the marketplace was working. A computer manufacturer replaced a tire manufacturer, and those 650 old jobs were replaced with 2,400 new ones. When the company moved to Eau Claire, Hutchinson said the deciding factor was state government's commitment to a positive business climate. And the company's own internal studies showed that Wisconsin's workers compensation, income, sales, and real estate taxes were lower than those in competing states. If I had listened to the liberals, people in Eau Claire probably would not have those 2,400 new jobs, and I doubt they would still have the 650 Uniroyal jobs either.

Today, Wisconsin's economy is "whirring," according to

U.S. News and World Report. More people are working than at any time in our history. Our unemployment rate is at a twenty-five-year low, and two full points below the national level. Wisconsin's economic turnaround stands as a real-world example of how a proactive state government can help create more jobs and opportunity for workers and their families. In fact, our biggest challenge today is a shortage of workers to fill the jobs our economy is producing.

As we approach a new century, America needs to redefine the relationship between business and government. The prevailing adversarial posture is based on political and economic dogma of a bygone era. Wisconsin demonstrates that with all the labels stripped away, people can see the private sector for what it is: the engine that provides jobs and opportunity for people. Government has a role in checking the engine; enforcing speed limits, rights of way, and safe passing; and preventing hit-and-runs. Its central role, however, should not be to set up roadblocks, detours, and tollbooths every half-mile on the road to economic growth.

If American government does not evolve toward a new partnership with the private sector, jobs will be created elsewhere. Wisconsin provides a case study. High taxes and unreasonable regulation pushed businesses out of Wisconsin. Lower taxes and regulatory relief helped bring them back. As the national economy becomes increasingly global, American businesses will look to the bottom line when deciding where to locate and grow their enterprises. America needs a tax and regulation overhaul, and a new attitude in government, to keep those jobs here.

CHAPTER SEVEN

PROTECTING THE ENVIRONMENT

I made waves when, in my first inaugural address back in 1987, I talked about the importance of protecting the environment. As one newspaper reporter wrote, "Thompson surprised observers at the noon ceremony in the capitol rotunda by highlighting his commitment to preserving the state's natural resources."

It was the labels again. I was Republican, and a conservative one at that. The campaign was over and we had won. Why on earth would I say something like, "The greatness of Wisconsin comes from its natural resources, the abundance of beauty, its water, its wildlife, and its countryside" or "A clean environment is good business"? Republicans are stereotyped to be anti-environment. If you're pro-business, you must be anti-environment, the labels say.

I had a different view. I had grown up hunting and fishing, as many people in Wisconsin do. I took my son and my daughters with me, as many people in Wisconsin do. I had worked on farms as a boy growing up in Elroy. I enjoyed and respected Wisconsin's lakes and crisp clean air as much as any liberal or Democrat did, and I wanted to preserve that priceless heritage for my children and grandchildren—and for theirs. (I often tell people, "Minnesota brags about having 10,000 lakes. We have 13,000 lakes, and ours have fish in them.")

Just as I was not willing to concede Progressivism to the liberals, I was determined to show that environmental stewardship and economic development are not mutually exclusive. And I wanted to make it clear to Washington that the people of Wisconsin could manage their environment just fine without federal mandates.

Wisconsin has a long heritage of environmental action. Before Gaylord Nelson, a U.S. senator from Wisconsin, established the nation's first Earth Day in 1970, Wisconsin was a national leader in protecting the environment. The nation's first environmentalists were conservationists like John Muir and Aldo Leopold from Wisconsin, and President Teddy Roosevelt. By and large, the conservationists were not liberal or conservative, Republicans or Democrats; they were farmers mostly, and outdoorsmen, and just ordinary citizens, who saw protecting the environment as a moral and commonsense responsibility. And from their concern and hard work, Wisconsin began to establish laws to protect the environment, before most other states or the federal government saw it as a major concern.

And so, just as Wisconsin served as the nation's laboratory for Progressive reforms in the early 1900s, our environmental laws became models for the federal government when Richard Nixon established the Environmental Protection Agency (EPA). Over time, though, Washington's good intentions have gone awry, as an army of EPA regulators seeks to impose its one-size-fits-all environmental solutions on every state and community across America.

Wisconsin has its own Department of Natural Resources (DNR), responsible for enforcing Wisconsin's environmental regulations and our fish and game laws. When I was first elected governor, DNR was not part of the governor's cabinet. Its secretary was appointed by an independent management board and was answerable to that board. Although the members of the board were appointed by the governor, subject to confirmation of the state senate, the governor had no direct authority over the secretary or DNR staff. Over time, as governors came and went, many DNR staff developed their most enduring relationships with environmental groups, which were the agency's most organized, influential "constituents." And DNR board members—who served on a part-time basis—largely were dependent on DNR staff for the information they needed to make their decisions.

Although the initial purpose of DNR's independent status was to insulate it from politics, the effect was to insulate it from being accountable to the citizens who crossed its path. In the northern part of Wisconsin, where fishing and hunting are a way of life, DNR was commonly referred to as "Darn Near Russia"—there were even bumper stickers saying this on the cars I saw as I traveled between towns. Many people felt DNR was too autocratic. It had broad authority over hunting, fishing, and land use and yet was not directly accountable to voters or their elected state and local representatives. It wasn't responsive to people. I remember talking to a farmer in the southern part of the state who had a problem with beavers on his land. They were building dams and flooding his field. His common sense told him to shoot the beavers and dynamite the dam, but that would have violated DNR regulations, so he did the right thing. He called DNR. Several weeks later, the beavers were as busy as ever, and the field was disappearing under water. All he could do was watch and shake his head.

My first response to the farmers and the people who thought of DNR as "Darn Near Russia" was to propose making it a part of the governor's cabinet. I wanted to participate in its dialogues, and I wanted it to participate in the broader discussions that included jobs and economic growth. That idea was shot down quickly and ferociously, and I learned it was too much too soon. Environmental groups liked the system the way it was. They had built strong, special relationships with the DNR bureaucracy, and they didn't want elected officials, particularly a governor, messing around with the system and diminishing their clout.

On the other side of the equation, I was hearing from small and large business owners who were pulling their hair out over the attitude of DNR bureaucrats. It wasn't that the business people—most of them anyway—disagreed with our environmental laws, it was that state government workers didn't seem to care about helping them figure out how to comply with the laws and still make a profit. The regulators were myopic. Their view of protecting the environment was "just say no" to businesses and property owners.

In 1987, I created a new Office of Business Advocacy, in the Department of Development, which could intervene on behalf of business people who were having trouble dealing with DNR and other state agencies. I also established a toll-free hotline for businesses looking for assistance and guidance in dealing with the state. In the first two years of operation, the hotline received an average 250 inquiries each month. There were real people out there, who previously had nowhere to turn for help.

We began taking a more balanced approach toward what had been perceived as polar opposite interests of business and environmentalists. Bruno Mauer, the secretary of development, established a dialogue with his counterparts at DNR—a regular sharing of information. That hadn't happened as frequently under the state's either-or approach. Sometimes—and any time is too frequently—we found private businesses doing things that were damaging to the environment. In those cases, we stood firm. If they were caught violating our laws, we didn't hesitate to fine them or prosecute them. But in many other cases, the situations were less clear-cut. We weren't letting the offenders slide, but we learned that when we brought DNR enforcers and private industry together, they actually started working together—both sides learned more about how to protect the environment—often without penalties or loss of jobs.

Attitudes began to change—we were seeing cooperation instead of confrontation. DNR was resistant at first, but when its people saw I wouldn't stop pushing them, they decided it was better to walk together rather than fight me. And so when individuals or businesses came to me with an environmental problem—like the company in La Crosse that wanted to build an expanded headquarters—I brought them to the table with DNR to try to work out solutions that achieved both their goals. It didn't always work, but often it did. It is amazing, really, how the labels start to disappear when people actually sit down together and work as partners. You tend to solve more problems and lessen tensions and stereotypes in the process.

Wisconsin's environmental groups weren't sure how to handle my pro-environment stance. To some, the fact that I was not anti-growth or even anti-capitalism closed the door to working together—they were too much invested in the labels. Other groups decided to take me up on the issue, to see if I really was the genuine article. In 1988, Cliff Messinger, a board member of the Nature Conservancy, a nationwide environmental advocacy group, talked to me about setting up a fund, with state dollars, to purchase and preserve environmentally sensitive land. To his surprise, I agreed—here was a perfect example of government playing an active role to protect the environment without enacting a whole new set of regulations and hiring more regulators to enforce them. I began working with the legislature to set up the fund. The legislature wanted a $500 million endowment. I met them halfway and signed into law a $250 million Stewardship Fund. Not bad for openers.

Since we started the fund, we have worked with nonprofit groups like the Nature Conservancy, as well as with local governments and businesses, to purchase 107,000 acres of green space, riverbanks, and other environmentally precious land. The fund has financed more than 1,400 land purchases, including the two largest in state history—12,000 acres of the Turtle-Flambeau Flowage, and the 6,900-acre Chippewa Flowage. My role in these purchases was to work directly with the land-owners to get the best price possible for the state. I threw myself into it, negotiating back and forth, like dickering over a used car. These were good, basic Elroy skills, which paid off. Even my most persistent critics were forced to acknowledge our success. The *Milwaukee Journal,* which at the time was one of the state's most liberal newspapers and rarely complimented me for anything, wrote, "Governor Tommy Thompson deserves a good share of the credit."

In addition to signing legislation investing state resources in new approaches to environmental protection, I did things on my own—things I didn't need legislative approval for—to demonstrate to businesses and others that the state would continue to be an environmental leader. These were tangible steps that focused on results rather than rhetoric. I began working with Wisconsin's paper companies on a voluntary program to reduce air and water discharges from the state's pulp and paper industry. This was a partnership with state government based on mutual goals, not a new set of regulations. The fact that I was not "anti-business" helped us work together—we trusted one another and had the same goals.

Historically the paper industry had been a major polluter, discharging chemicals used in the pulping process and chlorine used for bleaching paper into the Fox River, which runs through the eastern part of the state and into Green Bay. For years, the Fox River was considered a "dead" river, unsafe for swimming or fishing. Then Tom Schmidt, president of the Wisconsin Paper Council, came up with a plan for reducing the water and air discharges of the state's paper plants. We announced the initiative—called the Pollution Prevention Partnership—and Tom worked closely with George Meyer of

DNR to hammer out an approach that would work best. In a series of back-and-forth meetings, DNR identified the harmful compounds the paper industry needed to reduce, and together, they came up with a strategy for getting it done.

As a result of this cooperation, Wisconsin's paper industry has reduced its air and water discharges by 30 percent since 1987, while increasing its production by 20 percent. And today the Fox River is safe for both people and fish. In fact, it is one of our best fisheries for trophy walleyes. And one of the best fishing spots is just down the river from International Paper's Nicolet facility.

I also wanted to increase government's use of recycled paper. I soon learned, to my dismay, that it was too expensive to purchase the recycled paper in the quantity we used. The price came down as the volume increased, but the state needed only so much paper. So I asked Jim Klauser, secretary of the Department of Administration (DOA), to find a way we could do it. He and his staff designed a multistate purchasing agreement under which Wisconsin and five neighboring states agreed to cut through our various procurement regulations and jointly purchase recycled paper. This was the nation's first such multistate purchasing agreement. By joining together, we were able to purchase the paper at a volume-discount price. Together, we buy more than 30 million pounds of recycled paper a year. The paper we are saving otherwise would consume 560,000 square feet of landfill.

Through DOA I also launched a major initiative to conserve energy in state government. In 1990, EPA established a Green Lights Program to encourage states to conserve energy. I thought it was a good idea, but I didn't want to become even more entangled in Washington's bureaucracy. So I asked Bob Brandherm, the administrator of DOA's Division of Facilities Development, and Craig Weiss, our deputy director of engineering, to put together our own plan. They began meeting with state utility companies to get their ideas on how state government could conserve energy. They put together a plan, and a Wisconsin company, Johnson Controls, agreed to help us negotiate the best possible prices for new energy-saving equipment in state office buildings. Their proposal became the Wisconsin Energy Initiative, which has focused on basic changes like installing new lighting fixtures, steam traps, and other energy-saving technology in state office buildings—and creative approaches like using wastepaper fuel pellets in our state power plants. Burning paper fuel pellets alone has reduced state energy costs by 20 percent over the coal we had been using. The fuel pellets are made by small businesses in Wisconsin, using nonrecyclable paper that otherwise would end up in landfills. Instead of buying coal from out of state, we are producing more jobs for people in Wisconsin, reducing landfill refuse, and substantially reducing air emissions from our power plants.

We thought the initiative would pay back our initial investments in energy-saving technology within a six-year period. We've discovered that we'll recoup our investment within 4.8 years—it is remarkable how much energy can be saved by simple changes, such as using new, more efficient light bulbs in the exit signs of all state buildings. Over a ten-year period, the initiative will reduce state spending on energy by $60 million, and the annual environmental emissions will be reduced by 100,000 tons of carbon dioxide, 918 tons of sulfur dioxide, and 448 tons of nitrous oxides. In addition, we've helped create hundreds of new jobs in at least fifty Wisconsin companies that supply us with new energy-efficient products. Today, the state consumes less energy than it did in 1973, even though the square footage of our facilities has increased by 27 percent. In October 1993, we received the Domestic Energy Leadership Award from the United States Energy Association for this comprehensive conservation program.

Using alternative fuel in state cars was an idea that Jeff Knight, who ran our state car fleet, came up with as he was discussing our Energy Initiative with Jim Johnson and Leo Talsky, two other DOA employees. They discussed it with Secretary Klauser, he presented it to me, and I set up an Alternative Fuels Task Force to investigate what type of technology was available to begin experimenting with alternative fuels in state cars. We discovered that two Wisconsin companies could help us convert to natural gas–powered vehicles. A company in Milton could make the special carburetors, and a firm in West Allis was willing to make the special natural-gas cylinders to fit in the cars, but we needed someone to make the cars that could use the fuel. So we went to the General Motors (GM) plant in Janesville, and GM agreed to modify some of the trucks it was producing. We were getting cleaner-burning vehicles and providing new business to three Wisconsin companies at the same time.

As we proceeded with the natural gas experiment, I wanted to try other fuels and expand the limited program. I wanted to use ethanol, because I saw it as a way to open new markets for Wisconsin farmers, who grow corn that can be used to produce it. With Jeff Knight's help, I submitted proposals to GM, Chrysler, and Ford, asking if they would be willing to produce ethanol-burning cars for our experiment. GM called us back and said it wasn't sure if it could manufacture vehicles that could burn as much ethanol—85 percent—as we requested. Such a vehicle had not been manufactured before. An engineer at GM's alternative fuel division told Jeff that there was skepticism at the company. So I called Bob Stempel, the chairman and CEO of GM, and asked him to give it a try. We had worked together on job expansions at GM's Janesville plant. Bob agreed, but the state would have to help fund the research. I didn't want to use tax dollars for GM's research, so I asked the Wisconsin Corn Growers to start a fund-raiser to come up with the money, and with the help of the National Corn Growers, they raised the money for the research.

GM produced forty-eight of the "E-85" (85 percent ethanol) vehicles, which were the first of their kind in the world. Wisconsin's state auto fleet currently operates two hundred alternative fuel vehicles, which run on natural gas, propane, ethanol, or biodiesel (made from soybeans). By the year 2000, we plan to be operating 2,000 of these virtually nonpolluting vehicles. And in 1996, I announced Wisconsin's first ethanol plant, in Plover, which will produce the ethanol gas from cheese whey. (Once Wisconsin cheese gets into the picture, there will be no stopping us.)

When I served as chairman of the Council of Great Lakes Governors from 1989 to 1992, concern over pollution in the Great Lakes was a major regional and national issue. I worked with seven other governors of Great Lakes states to create a Great Lakes Protection Fund, endowed with contributions from each state. In my state budget, I asked for and received from the legislature funding for Wisconsin's $12 million contribution to the fund. I also appointed my predecessor, Tony Earl (who had served as DNR secretary before he was governor) to be Wisconsin's representative on the protection fund. The fund was a continuation of efforts begun in the 1970s by governors—Republicans and Democrats—working together to clean up the Great Lakes. This was not a mandate from Washington, but a cooperative effort by governors, municipalities, and businesses in the states that border the Great Lakes. Working together with a minimum of red tape, the states developed tough new water quality standards that helped reduce phosphorus discharged into the lakes from wastewater systems by 87 percent, and toxic levels in fish by as much as 90 percent.

Now, however, Washington has stepped in and is mandating a new set of water quality standards on the states as part of its own Great Lakes Initiative. EPA's 1,700-page initiative also prescribes policies we must follow to meet its standards. States like Wisconsin, which has one of the nation's most aggressive and comprehensive water quality programs, now must make costly changes in their own programs just to do it Washington's way, although there is no evidence its way will be more effective. Current and former Great Lakes governors of both political parties have protested EPA's arbitrary Washington-knows-best approach. As Tony Earl puts it, "Collaborative action rather than dictation from Washington, D.C., is the best way to maintain progress in cleaning and enhancing the Great Lakes." If only Washington would listen and learn instead of superseding grassroots solutions that are working.

In 1990, the Wisconsin legislature was engaged in a heated debate over establishing a law requiring businesses and local governments to recycle their trash. I supported the mandate, but wanted to make sure it was not just another regulation that government was going to shove down everyone's throat. I didn't think it would work unless the legitimate concerns of businesses and others were heard and addressed in the legislation.

The Wisconsin Newspaper Association, for example, told me its members were concerned because the legislation required them to print a certain percentage of their newspapers on recycled paper by certain dates. They didn't think they could make the internal changes in time to meet the deadlines, and even if they could, it wasn't clear whether there would be enough recycled paper in the marketplace for them to purchase to meet the requirements. So when the legislature forwarded the bill to me, I signed it into law. But before I signed it, I used my veto to change the percentages and timetables newspapers had to meet, because I understood the logistical problems they were facing.

I also vetoed a provision prohibiting grocery stores from using plastic bags, especially since there was no clear evidence that paper bags are environmentally superior. And I vetoed a provision banning a variety of products from being sold in Wisconsin because, according to the Wisconsin state legislature, their packaging was not environmentally sound. Wisconsin now had one of the most comprehensive recycling laws in the nation, but it was also more balanced than what I had received from the legislature. Since I signed the bill into law in 1990, almost every Wisconsin community has a recycling program in place. As a result, waste going into our landfills has been reduced by 25 percent. Again, we worked together to achieve a rational balance, and it's paying off.

I also worked with the legislature to develop a new approach to cleaning up environmentally sensitive land. The well-publicized failures of the federal government's Superfund program prompted state senator Mary Panzer, a Republican from West Bend, to lead an effort to establish an alternative approach. Wisconsin's Land Recycling program, which I signed into law in 1994, offers incentives for businesses to purchase and clean up contaminated land. Businesses were reluctant to purchase contaminated land because once they did, they became liable for pollution caused by others before they purchased it. Abandoned industrial sites were lying vacant and still contaminated, while businesses moved to suburban green spaces to expand their companies. The program changed that by eliminating liability for past pollution when a company buys contaminated land. In return for that release of liability, the purchaser agrees to clean up the site and receives assistance from the state for doing so.

Near Milwaukee, a large parcel of land sat abandoned and polluted from years of use as a tractor proving ground and repair shop. A business, Cellular One, was interested in building a warehouse in the area and contacted DNR about buying the site under our land recycling program. The company and DNR worked together to devise the best approach to cleaning up the land, and within four months, it was pollution-free and ready for building. The company now is constructing a new office building and warehouse on the site. People in the area have new jobs available, the community has a taxpaying business, and a parcel of polluted land no one wanted to touch is cleaned up.

In 1995, we went a step further. Many of the contaminated sites are located in low-income areas of the central city and slow-growing rural areas. I had established a development zone program to provide tax incentives for businesses to locate in such economically depressed areas, but those incentives did not address the barrier presented by contaminated sites. So I announced an expansion of the development zone program to provide an additional tax credit to companies that locate or expand to a contaminated site within a qualified development zone. If the company cleans up the site, it will receive a tax credit that equals 7.5 percent of its cleanup costs.

In 1994, a research group, the Institute for Southern Studies, released a report that substantiated what Wisconsin had learned during eight years of balanced pro-environment and pro-business policies. The group ranked all fifty states on environmental protection and economic growth, and then compared the two rankings. The study rated each state on twenty environmental measures, including toxic emissions, pesticide use, energy consumption, and spending for natural resource protection; and twenty economic measures, including annual pay, job opportunities, business start-up, and workplace injuries. Wisconsin ranked sixth in environmental protection and ninth in the strength of our economy. Only eight other states ranked among the top twelve in both categories. Bob Hall, the author of the study, said, "At a policy level, the choice is really not jobs versus the environment. The states that do the most to protect their natural resources also wind up with the strongest economies and best jobs for their citizens."

And people get the message. We rewrote our label to include pro-growth, pro-jobs, pro-business, and pro-environment. We're still putting all these objectives together to improve Wisconsin. Over the past decade, we have established new, comprehensive clean air and clean water programs, which are among the strictest *and* most effective in the nation. We have increased funding for pollution prevention incentives, such as a 205 percent increase in spending on our "nonpoint pollution" program, which prevents pollution on the farm and other places before it enters the water stream. We have eliminated 20 million old tires in four hundred stockpiles by helping businesses use recycled tires in their manufacturing process. Industrial pollution is down by 26 percent, and we've created more new manufacturing jobs than any other state. Our economy has created more than a half-million new jobs, and pollution discharges on land have been reduced by 53 percent, water discharges are down 51 percent, and air emissions are 24 percent less than when we started.

Elk and timber wolves are back in Wisconsin with the help of programs we started using new state funding in combination with private funds raised by foundations that worked in partnership with us. We have increased state funding for endangered species protection by 244 percent. For the first time since 1939, we built a new fish hatchery and upgraded two others under a $10.5-million program I initiated. And we have nearly doubled the miles of state recreation trails—primarily by converting abandoned railroad beds into a 780-mile state trail system.

Having a clean environment means so much more when people have the opportunity to ride a bike trail or get out on a lake to enjoy it. Being connected to nature is the essence of environmentalism—it is what motivated Wisconsin's first environmentalists, the conservationists. The one hundred timber wolves that now reside in Wisconsin and the one thousand eagles that nest here don't know what we've done to bring them back from the brink of extinction, but we do, and so will our children and our grandchildren.

I get a lot of satisfaction knowing that Wisconsin's record of environmental protection remains among the nation's strongest, but nothing can compare to the feeling I had when I released twenty-five elk into a northern Wisconsin forest in the spring of 1995. Elk had disappeared from the state 125 years ago, and now they are back roaming our forests. That is a real-life result, not mere rhetoric.

CHAPTER EIGHT

DRAWING THE LINE ON VIOLENT CRIME

I grew up in a community where individuals were held responsible for their actions. People were fair. They listened to your side of the story, but they turned a deaf ear to excuses. If you did something wrong, you paid the price. It was both the strength and integrity of the community, as well as the swiftness and certainty of the justice, that made Elroy a safe place.

In the 1960s and 1970s, with the visible tears in urban life, and in the wake of terrifying riots across the country, thinkers and elected officials refocused the political discussion of criminal justice issues on social causes. In 1967, President Johnson appointed a commission to study crime in America, and the report issued by the Kerner Commission became the benchmark by which criminal justice policy was created, measured, applied, and enforced. Wisconsin liberals embraced the recommendations of the Kerner Commission. The prevailing sentiment among many state legislators and criminal justice experts was that social and economic ills were at the root of violent crime. To prevent crime, one had to identify those injustices and overcome them. Social programs, they said, not prisons, were the answers to controlling crime. Perhaps the most compelling example of this view occurred in 1978, when the legislature changed the state juvenile code. The legislature rewrote the code so that its express purpose was to "remove" from the juvenile offender "the consequences of criminal behavior." Criminals in this sense were victims of their circumstances—a deprived childhood, racism, or abusive parents.

I entered public service with the belief that one of government's most fundamental roles was to protect law-abiding citizens from crime—providing safe neighborhoods where children and families can live, work, and play without fear. It was this commonsense understanding of government's role that drove my zero-tolerance approach to crime and my determination to change our out-of-balance criminal justice system.

As a young state legislator, I had proposed a new prison for serious offenders between the ages of sixteen and twenty-one. Wisconsin had no such facility. Instead, juveniles who had committed heinous crimes were lumped together with kids who got into trouble for tipping over outhouses or stealing bikes. This created two problems. First, juvenile facilities were like criminal training schools for young offenders who were not violent criminals. They learned more from the bad apples than they did from the state's efforts to "reform" them. And just as important, the serious offenders, the young thugs who were committing violent acts against others, were essentially getting away with it scot-free. A social worker and a donut was what kids got for committing serious crimes.

Construction on the new prison started in Oxford, which was located in my assembly district. In the fall of 1971, then-governor Patrick Lucey visited the site of the almost completed prison. It was scheduled to open with 540 beds the next year. I'll never forget it. As Governor Lucey stood outside the prison in the crisp autumn air, he said, "[T]his prison will never be opened." It never was, at least not by the state. In 1972, the governor sold the brand-new prison to the federal government for $13 million.

With each increase in the crime statistics, the governor and state legislature kept digging at the social roots of these problems, but not reaching them. It was the only approach they knew, but it wasn't successful. Between 1982 and 1984, serious crime in Wisconsin rose 6 percent, while it fell 12 percent nationwide. By 1985, the murder rate was up 16 percent, and rapes were up by 15 percent. Between 1981 and 1985, even though our population of young people was declining, the juvenile crime rate had risen 23 percent.

Wisconsin had not invested in prison space, so there was nowhere to put the growing number of violent criminals. And although the legislature had authorized the building of a sorely needed prison, Governor Tony Earl could not get it built. He wanted to build it in Milwaukee—because a majority of prisoners were from the city—on a site near County Stadium, home of the Brewers baseball team. But the citizens of Milwaukee didn't want a new prison in their backyard and put up a stiff fight.

By the standards of the day, Wisconsin's sentencing guidelines were commensurate with those of most other states. Governor Earl's criminal justice policy operated on the assumption that offenders were being properly dealt with as long as they were shown understanding, provided with good treatment, and given flexible prison terms in locations convenient to their families and acquaintances.

During the campaign, I worked with my advisers to prepare an issue paper on crime. We had to shift the balance of how the state dealt with crime. We would not rely on wishful thinking and hopeful theories to guide Wisconsin crime and prison policy. The criminal justice system needed to isolate and punish serious offenders, and provide rehabilitation programs to those who made credible efforts to use them. I proposed changing the state juvenile code to allow serious offenders to be treated as adults. I said I would build more prisons to keep criminals behind bars longer. And I promised to refocus state sentencing policies from treatment and parole to longer, "determinative" prison terms for violent offenders.

My opponents pointed out that prisons cost money. With all the vitally important things government has to do, they argued, we can't be throwing millions of dollars into more prison space. Their alternative: keep investing on the "front end" of the crime problem (meaning more government social programs) rather than on the "back end" (police, courts, and prisons). I was doing that too—with welfare reform, improving educational opportunities, and working to grow Wisconsin's economy and job force. For some reason, when I proposed those various programs, people failed to see how connected the pieces were. We had to take a holistic approach—and a tougher one.

The juvenile justice reforms I included in my 1987 budget were defeated in the legislature. Powerful liberal committee chairmen—like Representative Rebecca Young of Madison, who chaired the assembly Judiciary Committee—prevented them from even going to the floor. Instead they offered provisions preventing courts from detaining juveniles in a "secure facility" for more than forty-eight hours. Even conservative Democrat legislators had wanted the courts to be able to detain juveniles longer—for up to ten days. However, Representative Young squashed the reform, refused to consider the conservative Democrats' proposal, and wouldn't allow a vote on it. So these Democrat legislators came to me and asked me to use the veto to increase the forty-eight-hour limit in the bill. By striking three lines from the bill, except the letters that would spell out "ten days," I was able to change "not more than 48 hours" to "not more than 10 days." Democrat leaders were outraged, and dubbed it the "Vanna White veto." But the veto was more "democratic" than the legislative process had been, and there was no chance they could get a simple majority, much less a two-thirds majority to overturn it.

I visited most of the towns where Wisconsin's prisons were located during the campaign. In some places, the local people complained, but in others, they saw the prison as a part of their economy. In Waupun, where a maximum-security prison already existed, people wanted the additional beds, because it meant more jobs for their community. So during the campaign, I proposed that the existing prison there be expanded to add 650 new prison beds.

Soon after I was elected, though, Joe Strohl, the Democrat majority leader of the senate, announced that he wanted the new prison built in Sturtevant, a town in his district. The message from the majority leader was clear—the Democrats would oppose Waupun when it came to the floor. I saw the whole issue bogging down once again in a fight over where the prison should be built. It was exactly how Wisconsin had played prison politics for decades.

So I arranged for a town meeting in Waupun and spoke to about one hundred people in the municipal building gymnasium. I explained that I had to make a hard choice, and now I couldn't keep the promise I had made to them during the election. No prison would be built unless I agreed to build it in Sturtevant. Although people were disappointed, they understood how important the prison was in the state's attack on crime, and they gave me the green light. I went back to Madison and struck the deal with Joe Strohl. We submitted legislation establishing the new prison at Sturtevant, and forty-three days after I was inaugurated I signed it into law. The state building commission immediately began issuing bids for construction. Wisconsin was finally building the new prison.

Shortly after that, I decided to change the process for building prisons. Instead of the state deciding where new prison beds would be located, we would leave it up to the people. Communities that wanted new prison construction had to come forward and request to be selected. It didn't take long before mayors and city councils saw that new construction could be an economic benefit to their communities. The communities that didn't see it that way didn't ask for new beds.

I continued to spar with the legislature over adding more prison beds. In 1988, George Bush's campaign ran its now-famous "Willie Horton" ad. In Wisconsin the ad was a wake-up call for many legislators: people wanted tougher policy on crime. They weren't going to forgive public officials whose policies didn't protect them. For many Democrat legislators, it was no longer an issue of whether we needed prisons, but a question of how many. As a result, we've more than doubled our prison capacity since 1986.

With the political debate shifting and the pendulum swinging, we have been able to pass key legislation to change our sentencing laws—ideas I had been urging before catchy phrases like "three strikes" were even on the radar screen. Wisconsin abolished mandatory release laws, eliminated the "no consequences" language of the juvenile code, toughened our statutes on sexual predators, and introduced "life means life" to prevent judges from establishing any possibility of parole for murderers sentenced to life in prison.

Our court system also needed an overhaul—just like welfare and other government programs. Delays in resolving cases were wasting taxpayers' money, and crime victims were spending up to a year of their lives, missing work and wasting their time, waiting for their cases to work their way through the court system. So we speeded things up. I provided state funds to Milwaukee for the city to design its own system to eliminate delays in criminal prosecutions. The city established speedy trial courts, each of which only handles cases in a narrowly defined area of the law. They are far more efficient than traditional court systems because they learn one area of the law very well. We started with drug cases in 1990. In 1991, we added funds for homicide courts, and in 1992, we established speedy trial courts for sexual assault cases. With these new courts, the length of time it takes to resolve homicide cases dropped from an average 321 days to 92 days. And the average processing time for drug cases dropped from 307 days to 70 days.

Several studies—by the Brookings Institute, Harvard University, and the Wisconsin Policy Research Institute—have demonstrated the link between expanded prison capacity, longer sentences, and reduced crime in Wisconsin. It's not particularly difficult to figure out that keeping criminals in prison reduces crime. Punishment is effective crime prevention.

There are dangers too, though, in taking the get-tough approach too far. Like anything else government does, fighting crime requires a balanced, comprehensive, commonsense approach. Just as all prisoners should not be released automatically after serving only a part of their sentences, neither should all of them be locked up forever. Treatment programs can help people get their lives in order, and they do play a role in crime deterrence, but in conjunction with, not as a substitute for, law enforcement.

In the spring of 1991, Democrat representative Dave Travis formed a committee to recommend cuts to my prison expansion plan. The committee had some other ideas and recommendations. I remember meeting in my office with Christopher Mohrman, Bill McCoshen, and other members of my policy staff, trying to figure out a strategy. Morhman advised me to go to war, and we were getting ready to do battle, prepared to discuss the Democrats' ideas as more of the same old thing that failed before. Afterward, I thought it over on my own. The bottom line was that we needed more prisons. No committee could convince me otherwise—but why not hear what they had to say?

When we sat down, the committee introduced the concept of intensive sanctions. At that point, judges in Wisconsin had two options. They could sentence offenders to prison or to probation. Intensive sanctions would give the courts a third choice: a period of control and custody, highly supervised by the state Department of Corrections.

On one hand, the program offered punishment for nonviolent offenders who would otherwise occupy prison space needed for more serious criminals. But on the other hand, I didn't want it to be considered as an alternative to prison for offenders who posed a danger to society. The ratio of nonviolent offenders to violent offenders varies widely from state to state, but in Wisconsin, 70 percent of our current inmate population has committed some form of violent crime. And of the remaining inmates convicted of lesser drug or property offenses, a large share are either concurrently serving time for violent offenses or have a prior record of one.

I was very concerned that the original proposal allowed too many offenders into the program, and I felt uneasy about the impact on public safety. So I instructed my staff to draft amendments, which were adopted, to restrict the number and type of offenders who could participate in the program. Only those convicted of nonviolent or non–drug trafficking crimes would be considered; the traditional sentence the offender faced would be no more than three or four years; and above all, the offender must not have demonstrated a risk of violent behavior or pose a danger to the community.

Work is the primary "rehabilitative" component of the program. Offenders have to work to pay restitution to their victims, and they also have to pay the state a portion of the cost of running our intensive sanction program. Drug and alcohol testing and treatment, mental health services if necessary, and community service are all part of the program. If you fail to meet the requirements, you lose the privilege and are sent to prison. More than 1,500 Wisconsin offenders are under intensive sanctions, and the number is projected to increase by approximately 28 percent annually.

Clearly, intensive sanctions are providing more protection to the public than either probation or parole. Wisconsin's per inmate cost for intensive sanctions is more that double the national cost of electronic monitoring programs and seven times greater than our expenditures for parole and probation. Yet, at an annual cost of about $9,000 per offender, the program represents a substantial savings from the average incarceration cost of $21,000.

Although our experiment with intensive sanctions has demonstrated some success, the jury is still out on how much it can be expanded without abdicating government's fundamental responsibility to keep violent and potentially violent criminals out of our communities.

In the same way that we embarked on an experiment with lesser controls over the least violent offenders, we also argued for a program of even more intense control over our most violent convicts. In my 1995 budget, I proposed a new five-hundred-bed "Supermax" prison. In my view, we needed a place to put the most hard-core, incorrigible criminals, to separate them from the other offenders in our maximum-security prisons. Although a few legislators argued that we should build more "conventional" beds instead of the more expensive "Supermax" beds (which was an indication of how the politics of prison construction had changed since I was elected in 1987), the proposal passed the legislature in May 1996. The next step will be to choose a site and get it built.

We've done a lot of amazing progressive things in Wisconsin, but we haven't won the war on crime. Not yet. I can't say we've ended crime as we know it. I wish I could. We have made some remarkable strides reducing crime and changing people's attitudes about how best to control it. Yet, when I was running for a third term in 1994, an editorial in a Wisconsin newspaper disparaged politicians in general and me in particular for concentrating on "punitive crime control legislation that wins elections instead of comprehensive preventative measures." I don't think it's wrong to do what voters want, if it makes sense. I don't understand how creating jobs, improving education, ending welfare, beefing up law enforcement, expanding prison capacity, and intensifying penalties—how all these elements in combination—isn't comprehensive.

No one in Wisconsin is resting on his laurels after a hard-fought struggle. I'm certainly not. As with many of our reforms, we have transformed our criminal justice system into one that demands individual responsibility. As long as we continue to hold individuals responsible for their crimes instead of making excuses for them, I am confident our crime rate will continue to decline. And I'm still listening and coming up with my own ideas.

In 1996, the prisons in the state of Wisconsin began contracting with private companies to have inmates perform work that no one else in the private sector will do. Soon we expect prisoners in Wisconsin to be working to pay 25 percent of the cost of operating our adult prisons. In my mind, I can envision a completely different prison system. I would like to turn Wisconsin's prisons into factories—where all the prisoners are working. In many ways, it would parallel our W2 welfare reform, by which people who had been simply sitting around waiting for welfare checks are matched with levels of work they can perform. It could work the same way with prisons—with a few necessary precautions—where inmates would work all day, every day, instead of sitting in their cells. Good work would be rewarded, and poor performance, violence, and bad behavior would be punished—with Supermax. At night and on weekends, prisoners could take classes or receive treatment for alcohol or drug dependency, or psychological counseling.

There's always been something counterintuitive about criminals lounging behind bars at the cost of $300 million a year of taxpayer money. Working-class people had every reason to be upset about their tax dollars going to support welfare recipients capable of work. Now that we've eliminated welfare, I believe they have every reason to expect prisoners, people who committed crimes against society, to earn their keep.

But there's more to this idea than that. I believe in work. It's an acknowledgment of responsibility. And it might just be the best preventive measure around.

CHAPTER NINE

RESTRUCTURING GOVERNMENT

In any organization—but in particular in government—there is strong internal pressure to protect the status quo. Those who benefit from the way things are try to keep them that way. Government employee unions, incumbent politicians, and civil service protections combine to present a formidable barrier to change. Simple things, like rewarding good workers and firing bad ones, are very difficult.

When I was first elected, I promised I would "run state government like a business." I wasn't thinking of IBM, I was thinking about the grocery store in Elroy. Our profit margin at the store was very small, and we had to run a tight ship. Managing money and keeping track of inventory were top priorities. And we had simple commonsense rules. First and foremost, you had to please the customer. You had to deliver a good product at a reasonable price. If the customers weren't buying, it meant you didn't have the right product or your prices were too high.

After I mastered my first job in the store—sweeping the floors and cleaning chicken droppings off the eggs we purchased from area farmers—I was promoted to inventory. I took inventory once a week so we could put in an order for the food we needed. I couldn't skip a week, because food is perishable and we had to move it in and out of the store fairly quickly. We were a small store and we couldn't waste shelf space. If customers weren't buying a particular item, it didn't stay in the store long.

Later, when I was elected to the state legislature, I saw that state government ran somewhat differently. The idea of pleasing the customer—the taxpayer—was almost irrelevant. It didn't seem to matter whether government taxes—the prices charged to customers—were too high, or whether the "products" government was "selling" were inferior. The government was the only business in town. If customers didn't like the prices or the product, they had nowhere else to go. I earned my reputation as "Dr. No" in the state assembly by opposing government spending programs that didn't match my grocery store standard of doing business.

When I became governor, one of the first things I noticed was that no one in state government was in charge of taking a regular inventory of our products, services, and cash flow. Much of government seemed to be on automatic pilot. I was frustrated to learn that we didn't have a very good system in place to determine how much money was coming in and how much money was going out. Periodically, the state checked to see how the money flow was going, but not as carefully as my father had done in his small-town grocery store. The checkups were too infrequent to make adjustments, to ward off a shortfall or plan wisely for a surplus. As a result, the decade before 1987 was marked by a series of peaks and valleys in state fiscal policy. The money would go out, the money would come in. Someone would say, "Oh-oh, we've got trouble, the revenues aren't coming in as fast as the money is going out." So the governors—Republicans and Democrats alike—would call a special session of the legislature and raise taxes because of some unforeseen economic downturn that was drying up revenue to the state treasury.

It was the same with unexpected surpluses. The economy would pick up, and after a while someone would notice the state was in the black. So the governor would call all the legislators back into session and the state would decide how to spend the extra money. It was a feeding frenzy among state legislators vying for special projects. And in that kind of environment it didn't seem to matter that six months later they might all be back in another session to raise taxes again to meet another unexpected deficit. It was no way to run a government, or a grocery store.

We began to monitor every month exactly how much was coming into state government and how much was going out. Now when we see revenues slacking off somewhat, we can take action to avoid a crisis down the road that would prompt calls for more revenue from taxpayers. We slow down on government travel. We slow down on filling vacant positions. We slow down on staff promotions and other spending. And by the same token, we can tell whether revenues are coming in at higher levels than expected because of strong economic growth, and avoid the peaks and valleys. We can then plan accordingly, filling vacant positions as we go along or setting aside money for other purposes later. It's basic money management I learned in my father's grocery store.

In the months after the election, Jim Klauser and I shared a car to work most mornings. As we drove down East Washington Avenue in Madison, we passed row upon row of cars in huge parking lots. When I commented one morning on "all those cars," Klauser said, "You know those are ours." "Ours?" I asked. "What do you mean?"

"They are all state-owned cars."

"You're kidding." I said.

He wasn't.

The next morning, it snowed. And in the days that followed, those cars stayed in the huge parking lots. Every morning we drove by, and the cars just sat there with snow still piled on top of them. No one even cleared it off! It was obvious the state had too many cars that weren't being used. So I asked Jim to look into it. And it turned out, no one had ever taken an inventory. When we did, I learned the state had 6,617 cars assigned to various agencies.

We also found out that no one person in state government was in charge of all the cars. Each agency kept track of its own and used them in its own way. Many agencies couldn't even account for all their cars: they didn't know how many they had, exactly what they were being used for, or who was using them. Plus, our simple research revealed the state was paying more than $65,000 a year to rent the parking lots for the cars to sit in. We also discovered, not surprisingly, that everyone always wanted a new car. So the state was continually buying new cars to park in the parking lots, rather than keeping the cars it had well-maintained and in operation longer.

So I tried a commonsense grocery store solution. We consolidated the cars under one fleet and hired someone to keep track of them. We found an old state building that wasn't being used and housed the fleet there, out of the elements, and canceled the $65,000 per year parking lot leases. We beefed up maintenance and raised the number of miles cars had to be driven before new ones were purchased. We began strictly monitoring usage, and if someone was abusing a car or using it for personal purposes, we took the car away. Through this consolidation and improved management, we immediately reduced the fleet by 524 cars. Within a year, we had reduced new car purchases by 8 percent. To make this happen, we did have to hire a manager, as well as mechanics to keep the cars well maintained. But so far, we've saved $45 million on cars alone by using this commonsense management approach.

Secretary Klauser and his staff also did an inventory of the state's computer and phone systems. We discovered a situation much like the state-owned auto system: a cobbled-up mess. State agencies jealously guarded their own turf. Each agency wanted to have as much control and independence as possible, so there was no uniform system or standard. We had four excellent mainframe computers, but none of them could communicate with one another. There were also several different phone systems. So we put all the state agencies on the same phone system, consolidated computers, and established a uniform standard and computer language so agencies actually could communicate with one another. All this meant investing heavily in new technology, at a real cost. But again, it has paid off in the long run. We are saving more than $10 million every year in computer costs alone.

Making these changes sounds simple enough, but there was enormous bureaucratic resistance. It sometimes required persuasive action on my part to convince state agencies to change. The University of Wisconsin college system, for example, was dead-set against putting its cars under a state fleet. When I requested an inventory of the autos the university was using, I was told it would take months, and I shouldn't hold my breath. But soon after, the university requested some additional funding in the state budget. I mentioned the "car situation" in a way that suggested the cars and the funding were somehow connected, and within a couple weeks, we had a comprehensive list of all the cars, ready, willing, and able to join our consolidated fleet. (The university even found one of its cars in Africa.) The university felt the same proprietary way about its phones. It fought tooth and nail to avoid hooking into our phone system. This was a typical bureaucratic turf battle. After all, it was the *university*; it needed its own separate phone system. After a prolonged period of arm-twisting, it finally gave in. Now we're saving more than $1 million a year because of the consolidation.

These are the kinds of bureaucratic victories most politicians like to tout. Although one or two of these changes by themselves often didn't amount to a huge savings within the context of the total state budget, every little bit counts. And combined, they add up to hundreds of millions in savings each year for taxpayers. My feeling is, they're nice battles to have won—but they're not the Revolutionary War. As we continued to push state agencies to extract more operational efficiencies, it became clear that management changes were only part of the solution. Changing the actual programs of state government— the broad policies we were pursuing in welfare, education, job creation, and cutting taxes—were having a much greater impact on restructuring government.

For example, when I set out in 1987 to change welfare, my goal was not to restructure government. I wanted to change welfare policies that were preventing people from becoming self-sufficient. So we worked with the legislature, and sometimes fought with it, on a policy front to pass Learnfare, Workfare, and other reforms that changed what government was doing to try to help people on welfare. After we had implemented several welfare reforms, it became clear that there were structural impediments to helping people on welfare find work. The way government was organized made sense under the old welfare model—we were very good at sending out checks—but it didn't make sense under the new model. We didn't have an efficient, coordinated system for helping people find work. So the welfare offices and the duties of welfare workers began to change—not by shoving "reinventing government" down their throats, but in an evolutionary way that made sense as we were trying to implement the new policies we had established. As the mission of government changed, the operation and structure of government followed.

This was also made clear once we started implementing new pro-business policies, and more actively promoting private sector job growth. We started making links between what our Labor and Development departments were doing and what our Welfare Department was doing. As we began working more closely with businesses, employers told us they had jobs for welfare recipients, but they didn't know how to locate them.

Meanwhile, welfare recipients were telling our welfare workers that they wanted to work, but couldn't find jobs. People looking for work and employers looking for workers were like ships passing in the night. So we established one-stop job centers throughout the state. Instead of bouncing around various government agencies, employers, welfare recipients, training and education specialists, and anyone looking for work or employment assistance now can find everything they need in one place in their communities or, today, on-line. The effect of the one-stop job centers was to downsize duplicative government efforts while providing better service to match up available jobs with people looking for work. The policy changes we implemented in the first instance created the impetus for the commonsense reinventing of government.

Milwaukee is the largest city in Wisconsin, eighty miles east of the capital. Like many large American cities, it has too many low-income neighborhoods, primarily located around the central city. From my first days in office, the problems of Milwaukee—poverty, crime, failing public schools—took a good part of my time and energy. I wanted to help people there realize the opportunities that other people in the state were enjoying. We passed welfare reforms. We started a job-ride program to help inner-city residents get to and from jobs in suburban areas. We started low-income home loan programs and minority business loan funds, and established development zones to encourage companies to locate in the inner city. As these new initiatives started to work in the field, we discovered something very interesting. The various state agencies responsible for implementing each of the reforms—the departments of Health and Social Services, Transportation, Labor, and Development, and the Wisconsin Housing and Economic Development Authority—were located outside the inner city, and most of them were not working together.

Welfare recipients trying to get back on their feet, entrepreneurs willing and able to start businesses in their own neighborhoods, and low-income families trying to buy their first homes had to trek across town or out to the suburbs to different agencies to take advantage of the new services and assistance we were providing. So we moved staff from six different state agencies into the central city neighborhoods we were trying to help. We put them all under one roof, and consolidated the various reforms into a comprehensive Central City Initiative. It was a simple, commonsense solution that no one had thought of before we began implementing the policy changes in the field. On their own, the agencies wouldn't have organized, because unless you saw the whole picture, not just the separate parts, you wouldn't have seen any reason for it. But once we passed and started trying new government policies, the old structure made no sense. Since we made the restructuring changes in 1991, the program has placed 932 people in jobs paying an average $7 per hour, made 324 home loans, and provided start-up capital to forty-three minority-owned businesses. In 1993, the national Council of State Governments selected the initiative for an Innovations Award, which recognizes "the best state programs and policies nationwide."

To many people, the savings we discovered during my first term seemed like reinventing government. They were smart, fresh looks at the bureaucratic system. They were getting at the problems from the bottom up. Then there was a gradual evolutionary process that flowed from our policy changes, from the top down. In 1995, we were jolted toward a far more expansive restructuring of government. During the 1994 reelection campaign, I was challenged to come up with $1.2 billion to increase state funding for the public schools—while simultaneously cutting property taxes—and I promised to do it without raising sales and income tax rates.

Even before I won reelection, state budget director Rick Chandler and his staff of budget analysts at the Department of Administration (DOA) began poring through the budget requests submitted by all the state agencies. They were trying to squeeze out all the efficiencies possible, looking to find the savings we needed. They were tireless and creative.

On November 20 and 21, Jim Klauser and I traveled to Williamsburg, Virginia, for the annual Republican Governors Association meeting. It had been a good election for Republicans. None of the ten incumbents up for reelection had lost, and fourteen new Republican governors were elected. Senator Bob Dole, who would be majority leader again, and soon-to-be Speaker of the House Newt Gingrich attended. Change was in the air, as Dole and Gingrich promised a new partnership with governors and the devolution of power from Washington back to the states. After a day of meetings, Jim Klauser and I sat down to discuss how my budget would pay for the $1.2 billion shift in school funding. We had talked before about going beyond the numbers—about going "outside the box" of how government was structured. And we began to map out a strategy to reinvent government. We started from scratch. We didn't talk about numbers. What would government look like in Wisconsin if we could, in effect, start over? How would we restructure it to best achieve the policies state government was pursuing? Maybe if we took this approach, the savings would reveal themselves.

I must admit to having been very skeptical of the whole reinventing government game. Politicians like to promise it, but can't provide a compelling reason to make the change. All businesses, for example, would like to be smaller—but unless you show them that they can deliver the product more efficiently that way, there is little incentive or appreciation for the suggestions. Government is no different.

We identified the issues that were most important to me: moving people from welfare to work; improving education, jobs, and economic growth; juvenile crime; the environment. As we talked through each issue, we began to sketch a diagram—literally, on a piece of scratch paper—of what a new government might look like.

For example, in 1995, I was prepared to announce W2, our

replacement of welfare. It was going to be a jobs program, not a welfare program. So why did we need a welfare department? Wouldn't it make more sense to have a jobs department? We crossed out the state welfare division and transferred responsibility for W2 over to our Labor Department.

Education reform was going to be one of my top priorities during the next term. I was going to expand private school choice, establish tougher statewide education standards for public schools, and expand our school-to-work program substantially. But the Department of Public Instruction (DPI) was a major roadblock to change. Its "independent" status didn't make it more responsive to voters—on the contrary, it was controlled by the education establishment. The public was holding me responsible for improving our education system, but the state agency responsible for education wasn't even part of the governor's cabinet. So we crossed out "DPI" and wrote "Department of Education" under the governor's cabinet agencies.

We went down the list. Holding juveniles responsible for their crimes meant shifting responsibility for juvenile justice from our Department of Health and Social Services to the Department of Corrections. Creating more jobs meant consolidating economic development operations even more than we had, shifting responsibilities from various departments to a new Department of Commerce. And so on down the list.

After we returned from Williamsburg, Klauser presented our sketch to Rick Chandler and his team of budget analysts. They had a new mission. It wasn't enough to just look for spending cuts, now they had to turn our Williamsburg "map" into an actual budget that restructured government *and* achieved the savings we needed. For seven weeks we met together in a conference room at DOA, poring through the options. The assumptions Klauser and I had made in Williamsburg were challenged and rehashed in more than one hundred hours of discussions. In turn, I challenged the budget analysts to stop being so conventional, to think boldly.

The budget we produced restructured twenty-one state agencies and funded the property tax cut by cutting spending levels in thirty-three of forty-eight state agencies and reducing state employee positions by 3,000. On June 29, the legislature passed my budget with few major changes. Although the $1.2 billion property tax cut on the books created the impetus to make this happen, we were restructuring government to match the experience we had gained from eight years of field-tested policy reforms on every major issue government faces, from law enforcement to creating jobs.

Many recent attempts to change the way the federal government operates have received much ballyhoo, but have fallen short—from Ronald Reagan's Grace Commission to Al Gore's Reinventing Government.

The problem has to do with the way Washington has approached restructuring. Invariably, a special task force or commission examines the operations of government and proposes changes to make government smarter and more efficient. These reforms usually are announced with great fanfare, but after the public relations blitz subsides, the reforms inevitably grind to a halt in the political and bureaucratic process. Nothing significant really changes. The supposed beneficiaries of the revamped services find themselves no better off, and government continues to expand. Taxpayers are left wondering what really happened.

Politicians usually take the path of least resistance. Management changes at the operational level of government are important, and achievable to a point, but fundamental changes in government policies are much harder to accomplish. They expend energy and political capital. It is far easier to announce restructuring changes to satisfy the public's desire for more efficient government. But there is too much institutional resistance to achieve significant change that way.

Government can be shrunk and dramatically restructured to deliver better services for people. But reinventing government cannot happen in a vacuum. It must be based on fundamental policy changes and their real-world applications. If not, there really is no change.

Only changes in the underlying policies and programs of government will bring about fundamental changes in the structure and behavior of government. In Wisconsin, we changed the course of government policy. Restructuring wasn't simply a popular promise. It had become common sense. And when we were challenged, we didn't just spin our tires in ideological ruts—we made it happen.

CHAPTER TEN

MAKING IT HAPPEN

It's been a long time since people took state government seriously. All the talk in Washington about "devolving power back to the states" caught many across the country off-guard. "Give power back to the states?" I was asked quite often. "What for? What difference does it make?" As chairman of the National Governors' Association, I guess I should have been offended, but I wasn't. Like scientists in a laboratory, the other governors and I have kept our experiments kind of quiet—until we knew how well they worked.

For the last ten years in Wisconsin, we've been searching for solutions to a wide range of problems. Some government programs, like welfare and public education, were rooted in the best of intentions, but somehow lost their way and their sensibilities over time. Some challenges, like balancing the budget or encouraging growth in the economy, seemed perpetual. Conventional wisdom was, you could treat some of the symptoms, but no one really believed there was a cure to be found in our lifetimes. And other concerns, like the environment and crime, seemed to have grown in intensity during our lifetimes, with no solution in sight.

As governor, the official head of this laboratory of democracy, I've had to look not only at the individual problems, but
at the situation as a whole. And I knew, going in, there were
some tried and easy ways to quick-fix some of the problems—
but these would make other problems worse in the process.
That wasn't good enough.

My approach to solving problems did not spring up
overnight. Much of it came from my upbringing. I didn't wake
up one day and declare that individual responsibility would be
the base ingredient for my reforms. It was a value that was
inculcated in me by my parents, my school, my church, and my
neighbors in Elroy. My belief in proactive state government
didn't come from a political science textbook—this I learned
from watching a helpful, responsive, and solution-oriented government operate out of my father's store. My willingness to
experiment with new ideas and make government a positive
force for change did not emerge from hours in the library studying Wisconsin's Progressive tradition. It came from growing up
in a state where those Progressive values are unspoken,
accepted beliefs, handed down from one generation to the next.
Most people in Wisconsin don't know who national Progressive
leader Herbert Croly was, but, like me, they believe government should get the job done. If nothing else, that is
Wisconsin's Progressive tradition—responsive government
solving real-world problems.

I am sure that almost everybody in the state wanted to see
the same things accomplished: more jobs, less crime, lower
taxes, better schools, cleaner water, less dependency. There's no
way to count how many different ways, though, people thought
these things should be achieved. I've listened to most of them.
("Remember," my father said. "You have two ears and one
mouth. Use them in that proportion . . . ") Not all ideas I have
shared are mine originally. Bits and pieces and even major seg-
ments of solutions came from people I listened to. I've had the
benefit of a terrific team of visionary "scientists" working with

me. One of the very first things I did as governor was appoint "visiting professors"—talented people from outside government—to run key agencies. We're constantly being told that government is too complicated to be run by so-called outsiders or nonprofessionals. It is simply not true. And like all good governors, I've gained most of my insights from very compelling, creative experts in the field: the people of this state. We've learned how to make state government work, we've made it happen together.

Ronald Reagan once said, "They say the world has become too complex for simple answers. They are wrong. There are no *easy* answers, but there are *simple* answers. We must have the courage to do what is morally right."

Back when I had just been elected to my first term, I received a letter from a man in Brodhead, a small farming town in southern Wisconsin. He was, he wrote, fifty-one years old, had been married to the same woman for twenty-eight years, and was the father of four children who were now grown and off to college. He had served his country in the military, attended the University of Wisconsin, and was semiretired as a general contractor. He was active in his community, working on projects to revitalize the downtown and improve the airport to attract more business to Brodhead. He said he was neither a Republican nor a Democrat. When his friends asked him whom he was going to vote for, he wrote that he'd say, "I don't think it makes a difference who I vote for. They are all nice guys and they mean well, but after a few months of getting caught up in the machinery of government, they are all pretty much the same."

The real point of his letter, though, was that he wanted to tell me he thought I might be different. He had been trying to tune his television to the movie *Hell Is for Heroes*, but the reception wasn't very good, so he stumbled across me giving my first State of the State address. He closed his letter with "Let's get Wisconsin going."

I think we have.

The sentiment he expressed, I believe, is one shared by many Americans today, ten years later. Our frustration with government seems particularly focused toward Washington because the federal government is not solving problems. It's creating new ones. Washington seems like a distant and yet troublesome obstacle that needs to be worked around to get things done.

People, ordinary people, have a hard time being heard over the massive machinery of Washington—the grinding bureaucracy, the din of special interests, the partisan squabbling, and the clamor of the "inspectors"—the media. Sometimes, I think it really makes people who work in Washington hard of hearing.

I've learned that it is not so hard to listen when you are campaigning for elected office. Not only are you out there constantly shaking hands, you have pollsters and political advisers who can tell you exactly what percent of the population wants this or that. You can be responsive merely by talking about things—until you are elected. Then you are accountable, or you are supposed to be accountable, for getting things done. That is one thing Bill Clinton doesn't seem to understand—the difference between campaigning and governing. It is one thing to make promises that sound good to people and quite another to actually get them done.

Making it happen, making government truly effective, boils down to commitment and leadership. It means sticking with your ideas even when you're fighting an uphill battle, or taking a battering in the press. And when you think you've changed things, it means realizing that you're only part-way there. I hope this book will encourage people to expect more of themselves and of their states. I hope it will encourage more governors and legislators to try different things. Wisconsin's experience shows that when you have a good idea and the courage to stick with it—even if it's not politically popular at the time— you can change government for the better. Of course, you won't win every time. The only way you can be sure you never lose is to never try, but that isn't governing. It's self-protection and protecting the status quo in areas where it isn't working.

I've had to confront the labels that dominate so much of politics and government. A Republican wasn't supposed to care about helping people get off welfare. Cutting their benefits fit the label—but not investing more money in job training, child care, and health care. The labels said I couldn't be pro-business and pro-environment. And a small-town white Republican wasn't supposed to be concerned with the big-city problems facing black and Hispanic families in Milwaukee. The labels said I wouldn't go into the inner city and work to create jobs there, or join with low-income parents to give them the power to choose better schools for their children.

I am a conservative, but some of the things I did made conservatives mad. My solutions didn't always fit the doctrine of the Heritage Foundation, and I don't litter my speeches with all the buzzwords or the philosophies of Edmund Burke or Friedrich Hayek. When I was confronted with problems, I didn't check with the pollsters or hold up my solutions to an ideological litmus test. I did what I thought made common sense. I did what I thought would work, in my gut and in my heart.

Part of leadership is simply representation—reflecting what people want. It's not about following trends closely—it has to come from a belief in yourself and your abilities as well as a belief in people and their abilities.

But what does the Wisconsin experiment mean for the rest of the country? What works in Wisconsin, I'm told, can't possibly work in California, in Mississippi, or even in our neighbor, Illinois.

I disagree. The underlying *values* of our reforms and the *common sense* of them are universal. Basic principles such as work not welfare, parents deciding what schools their children will attend, holding criminals responsible, helping businesses create jobs, letting people keep more of what they earn, running government like a small-town grocery store—these are applicable across the board. They are not complicated solutions. But making them happen isn't easy.

I won't argue that every program that has succeeded in Wisconsin will work everywhere else in the country. Ironically, perhaps, that is exactly my point. States need to figure out for themselves what works and what doesn't. The process of discovery is what *Power to the People* is all about.

In his 1996 State of the Union speech, Bill Clinton said that "the age of big government is over." And yet nowhere in his ninety-minute speech was there a word about transferring any federal government power back to states and communities. Big government in Washington will never dismantle itself. The way government in America now operates will not change unless there is a fundamental shift in the balance of power between Washington and the states. Power to the people will not happen as long as Washington dominates.

When he was campaigning for president in 1992, Bill Clinton also said he wanted to end welfare as we know it. We watched that get chewed up in the machinery of Washington. It was a nice promise. In Wisconsin, not only did we end welfare as we knew it, we ended it altogether. Washington couldn't make it happen—but a state could! The fifty laboratories of democracy are working every day to solve problems with new ideas. And Washington is starting to take note. It can't help but see. More important, people are feeling the difference—there's so much that can be achieved at the state level, even at the community level, that Washington will never figure out.

We have a historic opportunity at hand to require Washington to devolve power back to the states and to individuals. If nothing else, the Wisconsin experience shows that this just makes common sense.

INDEX